Supercook's
DAY BEFORE
COOKBOOK

ENIGMA

This is a guide to each recipe's preparation and cooking

Easy ☆

Requires special care ☆ ☆

Complicated ☆ ☆ ☆

This is a guide to the cost of each dish and will, of course, vary according to region and season

Inexpensive ⓵

Reasonable ⓵ ⓵

Expensive ⓵ ⓵ ⓵

Time Guide — Dishes to Prepare the Day Before
The preparation and cooking time given for the recipes refers to the initial time it takes to prepare the dish. The serving time refers to the time necessary to complete the dish before serving; it includes cooking time where necessary.
This is a guide to the preparation and cooking time required for each dish and will vary according to the skill of the individual cook

Less than 1 hour ◿

Between 1 hour and 2½ hours ◿ ◿

Over 2½ hours ◿ ◿ ◿

Serving Time. The following is a further guide to the Serving Time required for each dish and will vary with the skill of the individual cook. It also includes re-heating or cooking time where appropriate.

Less than 1 hour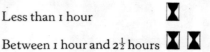

Between 1 hour and 2½ hours ⧗ ⧗

Time Guide — Dishes to cook in 30 minutes
This is a guide to the preparation and cooking time required for each dish and will vary according to the skill of the individual cook.

Less than 30 minutes ◗

Between 30 minutes and 1 hour ♨

Readers please note:
Equivalents for American ingredients are given in the text in square brackets. All weight and measure equivalents are approximate.
Tablespoons and teaspoons are Standard Spoon measures and are level.

Recipes and food preparation by Elaine Bastable, Shirley Nightingale, Frances Pratt and Jennie Reekie

Pictures supplied by Barry Bullough, Camera Press and Don Last

Illustrations by Jannat Houston

Published by Enigma Books Limited,
58 Old Compton Street,
London W1V 5PA

© Copyright Marshall Cavendish Limited 1973, 1977

This material was first published in
101 *Dishes to Prepare the Day Before* and
101 *Dishes to Cook in Thirty Minutes*

First printing 1973
Second printing 1977

Printed in Hong Kong

ISBN 0 85685 021 7

INTRODUCTION

Supercook's DAY BEFORE COOKBOOK will be a boon to everyone who has ever come home, late and tired, to the prospect of devising an appetizing meal that doesn't take long to prepare, as often as not when the cupboard is bare. Delicious and beautifully served food does not need to take hours to prepare and cook. Everyone – harrassed housewife, career girl or bachelor – knows the sinking feeling that accompanies the news that an unexpected guest has arrived at the end of a busy day. And everyone has experienced the dread of fixing – and eating – the same old meal again. So, here are almost 200 recipes that can either be cooked in half an hour or made in advance and served when they are needed. All the information that you will need is here, from basic recipes to hints on stocking a pantry cupboard, storing and freezing and tips on balanced, healthy eating. With Supercook's DAY BEFORE COOKBOOK you will be able to plan – and cook – ahead . . . the surest way to carefree and happy dining.

CONTENTS

INDEX OF RECIPES

DISHES
TO PREPARE
THE DAY
BEFORE

PLAN & PREPARE AHEAD

Any busy housewife – and especially one who holds down an outside job – will appreciate the time and energy savings of preparing and cooking meals ahead. And anyone who has ever come home late and tired, and has been faced with the preparation of a meal from scratch, must know from experience that the greatest cooking aid is a little forethought and planning! The recipes in this book have been planned so they may be prepared or cooked in advance – most can be cooked at least a working day ahead and some can be kept for weeks at a time – to enable you to avoid last-minute rush and unnecessary fuss.

Each recipe is provided with instructions for storage, followed in each case with the final steps needed before serving. You need not follow the storage instructions, of course, unless these include a necessary chilling period. If you wish to make the dish right away and omit the storing time, you may do so. But do not be tempted to store any of the recipes in ways other than those which are recommended, or for longer periods than have been stated.

At the beginning of each recipe a guide to preparation and cooking time for all 'pre-storage' stages is given, as well as a guide to the time required for stages just prior to serving.

Planning ahead

It will help enormously towards trouble-free cooking if you can manage to plan ahead as far as possible, and to know in advance the sort of dishes you will want to serve on certain days. Even if you are not the sort of person who can predict your life beyond the next 24 hours, it will help if, for a special menu, you plan to shop at least one day in advance. This way you can change your mind about certain ingredients or dishes if the ones you need are not available that week, or have suddenly risen in price. A well-stocked store cupboard will cut down on last-minute panics too; check the chart on page 5 for the basic foodstuffs it is sensible to buy in bulk, and those which will deteriorate rather quickly, and should, therefore, be bought in smaller quantities. Some foods may be stored at room temperature or in a cool dry place, some need airtight containers – and for others a refrigerator or freezer is necessary. Your own resources may well not include the full list of these facilities, but they are not *all* an essential pre-requisite of trouble-free preparation, and our recipes vary among them.

1. Kitchen and larder space

The old-fashioned larder, for so long a feature of most homes, is seldom found these days – and certainly not in modern buildings. Other space priorities tend to take precedence over this useful walk-in cupboard. Indeed storage space is so often at a premium that refrigerators are often utilized when they are not really needed. Eggs, for instance, may be stored in a larder for 2 to 3 weeks, and are frequently more immediately suitable for use when they are not refrigerator-cold: meringue mixtures will achieve a better volume,

and mayonnaise or butter-and-egg mixtures are less likely to end in curdling, if the eggs are at room temperature. If you have the space for one, an egg rack is a most attractive and practical kitchen extra.

Many cheeses, too, will benefit from being kept out of the refrigerator – again if you have the space for sensible storage. Brie, Camembert and Gorgonzola, for example, will not ripen under refrigeration (a useful point to remember if you need to keep any of these for a later date). Refrigerating bread is a common enough procedure – but do remember that the crisper loaves will go stale more quickly if they are refrigerated. Gâteaux and flans, such as those on pages 32 and 33, are better kept in a larder or other cool place once they have been fully prepared. And in the salad season, why not make up about ½ pint [1¼ cups] of French dressing in a screwtop jar: it will be ready for use as you require it – for up to 6 months.

2. Airtight containers

It is very important to ensure that an airtight container really does exclude air completely. If the lid of a tin or box seems not to fit as tightly as it should, put a layer of greaseproof [waxed] paper or foil over the top before adding the lid, to make sure a snug fit is achieved. (The same rule often applies to screwtop jars, as well.) Most of the cakes which store well in this way are the ones which contain moist ingredients which inhibit drying-out – treacle or molasses, honey, syrup, and fruit both fresh and dried. On the other hand, any crisp biscuits (such as the Ginger Snaps on page 57) will rapidly lose their texture if moist air gets to them during storage. The container you choose does not, of course, have to be a metal one – today many housewives prefer to use the more

modern plastic varieties designed especially for storage and available in many shapes and sizes. Dry ingredients used in cooking – flour, baking powder, salt, sugar, gelatine, and so forth – may be transferred to your own containers if you like to display these, and have the space to do so – but again these must be airtight ones. Remember too that jams and bottled fruits, however attractive they may look on display, will lose their colour and quality if exposed to light for long periods of time. These should be stored in a closed cupboard.

3. Refrigeration

Planning and preparing ahead allows you to use your refrigerator in a particularly sensible way. It takes, for example, no more time to prepare enough vegetables for two days as it does for one – and ready-prepared green vegetables will keep well for 24 hours in a plastic bag. Root vegetables, such as carrots and potatoes, may be scrubbed and peeled and kept in lightly salted water for 2 to 3 days, if you change the water every 24 hours. Ingredients for green salads may be washed and shaken dry (or dried on absorbent paper) and stored loosely wrapped for up to 5 days. If your refrigerator has a special vegetable container at the bottom, use that rather than the wrapper.
The same 'preparing-twice-at-one-time' rule also applies to pastry doughs, cake mixes, batters, and sauce bases. Keep an extra quantity of rubbed-in fat and flour in a container, ready for water to be added as required. Making mayonnaise is a fairly careful procedure and takes a little time and care – so make double the quantity you need; the rest may be kept well-covered for up to one month.
Most foods should be covered before refrigeration – either to stop their

surface from drying up, or to prevent any odours from transferring from one food to another (dairy produce is particularly apt to collect other 'tastes' unless it is always kept covered). Some foods, such as fresh fish and meat, should not be kept airtight because they tend to 'sweat': put these on to plates, and cover loosely with foil or greaseproof [waxed] paper. And cooked meats should be wrapped very well, but again must not be made airtight.
Always allow food to cool before it is refrigerated – putting hot food straight in will reduce the efficiency of the temperature controls, and may cause strain to the motor. If you particularly want a dish to cool fast (perhaps a gelatine mould which is needed in a hurry) cool it first by standing the container in iced water.
Although some breads are better not refrigerated, it can make a lot of sense to prepare bread and butter ahead – wrap it first in damp (not wet) absorbent paper, and then tightly in foil. It will keep for up to 12 hours. Breadcrumbs keep well in a covered container for up to 2 weeks: they are very useful for making stuffings and toppings, and are an excellent way of using up odd ends of unneeded loaves.

4. Deep-freezing cooked and made-up dishes

Wrapping materials
All food must be correctly wrapped, or packed, before it is frozen – except for items such as decorated gâteaux. These latter should be covered after the initial freezing, so that the decorations will not be disturbed by the wrapping. Whichever wrapping you use, be sure that it is completely airtight, covers the food completely, and that as much air as possible has been excluded. The presence of air inside the package can lead to 'freezer-burn', in which patches of food dry out and discolour. But do remember that water turning to ice will expand – and so a container for a water-based food must allow 'head-room' of $\frac{1}{2}$-inch for this to occur. Strong *polythene* [*plastic*] *bags* are excellent for all except liquids. They can easily be moulded around shapes to exclude air, and may also be used to line cartons or boxes. Be sure to use the correct weight of polythene sold specifically for freezing, and that you use specially-coated wire ties with them. *Moisture/vapour-proof film* is handy for some items, especially for the separate pre-wrapping of portions or individual parts of a larger package.
Plastic sheeting, sold in rolls, is also useful – again, though, make sure it is the correct thickness and weight or you may find it is easily damaged, and the food will leak and spoil.
If you use *aluminium foil* for wrapping, try to buy the freezer-weight foil, or use heavy-duty foil for both freezer and other wrapping jobs around the kitchen. If you use ordinary foil, do a double-thickness wrap to avoid the possibility of punctures.
Some of the best containers for packing food for the freezer can be found in the special *waxed cartons* and *plastic containers* now available. These are initially rather expensive, but have the

added convenience of being re-usable. They also pack well into the freezer cabinet, and of course are ideal for liquids, cooked foods, sauces, and so forth. The square or oblong ones use space more efficiently than the oval or round ones.

Sealing and labelling

Do not use ordinary adhesive tape for sealing packages for the freezer; this will not hold at the low temperatures which are involved. Special freezer tape should be used – around the edges of boxes and cartons, and to keep other wrapping secure.

Use special adhesive labels (again, the low temperature will not allow normal labels to hold secure) and write with a pencil, ballpoint or wax crayon – fountain pen ink will run. It is an excellent idea to colour-code foods: for example use red for meat, blue for fish, green for vegetables, yellow for desserts, and so forth.

Storage

Cool foods as quickly as possible before you freeze them – standing the container in a bowl of cold or even iced water will help. This precaution, together with the action of the 'fast-freeze' for newly introduced food in the freezer, helps to

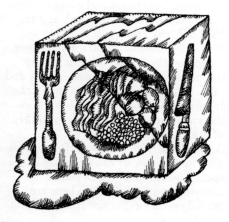

keep the food in a condition as near as possible to its pre-frozen state. Your freezer handbook will provide the recommendations on storage times for your guidance: for example, cream mousses are best if stored for only two months, as they will tend to dry out after that. Cooked meat and fish dishes are best stored for only four months: after that they will begin to lose flavour. It is sensible to remember that no food will improve in flavour or texture during freezing – but that there is no danger involved to health if you store frozen food for longer than the recommended time. The taste may deteriorate, but the safety in eating will not alter.

Freeze with caution

There are a few foods which do not freeze well; avoid these, and you will be spared later disappointment.

Mayonnaise will curdle if frozen – instead keep it in the refrigerator (see page 3).

Hard-boiled eggs will become tough and unpleasant to eat – so avoid any dishes which contain them.

Fresh *raw vegetables* cannot be frozen – they will become limp.

Jellies and other gelatine-based dishes run and 'weep'. If you are freezing mousses, make them up with $1\frac{1}{2}$ times the stated quantity of gelatine to prevent this from happening.

Thickened *stews or casseroles* should be made with cornflour [cornstarch] rather than ordinary flour – and use half the stated quantity. To prevent drying-out from occurring, add 1 tablespoon of oil to *pancake batter* if this is to be frozen.

Defrosting food

If you have time to allow food to defrost completely before it is reheated, you will generally obtain much better results. You are unlikely to encounter the possible disaster of serving a supposedly hot dish with still icy centre – and even if you are careful to re-heat

frozen food slowly, this may occur. The best way to defrost frozen food is in the refrigerator, still in its freezer wrapping. This will give the most uniform result and the best appearance. Defrosting may also be done at room temperature, if a faster method is needed.

If you are defrosting a dish which is to be served cold, you should allow approximately 24 hours in the refrigerator, or 8 hours at room temperature. If the dish is a particularly large one, allow 36 hours in the refrigerator, and 12 hours at room temperature. Do not try to get away with less time – allow a margin of extra safety if you can.

It is not safe to re-freeze food which has been defrosted without first cooking it. This is partly because the food will lose a great amount of its texture and flavour, but also because it may be dangerous to do so, in some cases. Partially defrosted food may occasionally be re-frozen, but since its exact state and temperature are not easily discerned, even this is not recommended.

5. Auto-timer cookery

Cooking auto-timed meals is an ideal practice for many occasions. If you are going out in the evening and want a hot meal waiting on your return, or if you spend an afternoon shopping, but need to cook a meal which will take some time, then an auto-timer copes efficiently in your absence. Many individual dishes, as well as complete meals, may be cooked in this manner, and you will be left free to pursue other activities.

Some dishes and meals are not suitable for this method of cooking, and there are a few simple rules to remember. But as long as these are followed and the necessary preparations made, there is no reason why auto-timing should not

become a regular part of your cooking.

A The dishes must be ones which can begin cooking from a cold state – and must not be ones adversely affected by remaining uncooked at room temperature for some hours. An uncooked flan case with a wet filling, for example, is not suitable for auto-timer cookery.

B The dishes must require no attention during the cooking time. A stew or casserole could be thickened, and the flavourings adjusted, just before the dish is to be served: anything which would require earlier attention may not be used.

C If a complete meal is to be cooked, all of the dishes must require the same length of cooking time, and the same oven temperature. Slight differences in heat of around 25°F can be allowed for: put the higher temperature dishes at the top of the oven, and the lower temperature ones at the bottom.

D Protect any foods which may discolour. Coat potatoes for roasting in melted fat, and cover vegetables for steaming or baking with water, or wrap in buttered foil.

E Add an extra 20 to 30 minutes on to the required cooking time, to allow for the oven to heat up.

Storage Chart

Food	Cool dry larder	Refrigerator	Freezer
Flours			
plain [all-purpose]	4-6 months	–	–
self raising	2-3 months	–	–
cornflour [cornstarch]	6 months	–	–
Raising agents			
bicarbonate of soda [baking soda]	12 months	–	–
fresh yeast	3-4 days	–	–
dried yeast	6 months	–	–
Eggs			
whole eggs	2-3 weeks	3-4 weeks	16 months (shelled)
whole yolks	1 day	4-5 days (in water)	2 months (with salt and sugar)
whites	1 day	1 week	6 months
hard-boiled	1 day	2-3 days	–
Fats			
butter	10 days	1 month	1 year
margarine	6 weeks	2 months	1 year
lard	6 months	1 year	–
packet suet	3 months	–	–
cooking oil	1 year	indefinitely	–
dripping	1 week	2-3 weeks	–
Liquids			
pasteurized milk	2-3 days	3-4 days	–
homogenized milk	3-4 days	4-5 days	2 months
sterilized milk (unopened)	1 week	1 week	–
single [light] cream	1 day	3-5 days	–
double [heavy] cream	1 day	3-5 days	2 months
stock	1-2 days	3-4 days	4 months
cream soups & white sauces (without meat)	1 day	2 days	4 months
Meat and Fish			
fresh joints	1-2 days	5 days	9-12 months
minced ground beef	–	36 hours	9-12 months
chops & steaks	1-2 days	1-2 days	9-12 months
offal [variety meats]	24 hours	1-2 days	2-3 months
fresh white fish	–	1-2 days	6 months
fresh oily fish	–	1-2 days	3-4 months
Desserts			
cream mousses	24 hours	2-3 days	2 months
jellies & gelatine-based desserts	24 hours	4-5 days	–
Made-up recipes			
rubbed-in cakes	2-3 days	–	6 months
creamed cakes	1 week	–	6 months
whisked cakes	1-2 days	–	6 months
rich fruit cake	3-6 months	–	–
shortcrust pastry (raw)	1-2 days	2-3 days	2 months
(cooked)	1 week	3-4 days	6 months
rubbed-in cake mix (fat & flour only)	2-3 weeks	3 months	
suet pudding mix (suet & flour only)	1 week	2-3 weeks	–

9

from left to right: top row: Mushroom Cocktail, Florida Cocktail, French Bean and Egg Salad, Chilled Melon and Pineapple
centre: Jamaican Grapefruit
bottom row: Globe Artichokes with Curry Mayonnaise, Roquefort Pear Salad

VEGETABLE & FRUIT FIRST COURSES

Vegetable Salads for Hors d'oeuvre
Many simple salads make excellent hors d'oeuvre as they are light, easy to digest and whet the appetite for the next course. They can be served on their own or as part of a mixed hors d'oeuvre. Good salads which make popular first courses are fresh tomato salad with garlic and basil; sliced, raw button mushrooms tossed in well-seasoned oil and vinegar; a coleslaw made from green and red cabbage, nuts, raisins and sour cream (or sour cream and mayonnaise mixed together); or potato and frankfurter salad made with cooked potatoes, apple, celery, green pepper and chopped frankfurters, bound together with mayonnaise flavoured with a dash of French mustard.

Peeling and Segmenting Citrus Fruit
Use a fairly small and very sharp knife, preferably stainless steel. Hold the fruit over a bowl to catch any juice, and cut off the peel with all the white pith, going from top to bottom in a circular movement. Some people find it easier to cut a slice from the top and bottom of the fruit, and then to place it on a board and cut downwards in sections to remove the peel and pith.
Segmenting should also be done over a bowl. Cut in towards the centre, inside the skin which encloses each segment, so that only the flesh is removed. Repeat this with all the segments, and then squeeze the pith and skin for any remaining juice.

Roquefort Pear Salad

☆   ①   ◫   ⧗

Preparation time: *15 minutes*
Serving time: *minimal*
SERVES 4

4 ripe dessert pears
lemon juice
2 oz. [4 tablespoons] **Roquefort or other blue cheese**
2 oz. [4 tablespoons] **cream cheese**
2 tablespoons mayonnaise (see page 63)
1 tablespoon chopped walnuts
a little single [light] **cream or milk**
salt and pepper

To garnish:
lettuce leaves
paprika

Peel and halve the pears, scoop out the cores with a spoon, and dip the fruit quickly in lemon juice to preserve its colour. Place on a serving dish.
Mash the Roquefort or blue cheese with the cream cheese and mayonnaise. Add the walnuts, then soften the dressing with sufficient milk or cream to give a coating consistency. Season to taste, and spoon the dressing over the pears.

Make a loose tent-covering of foil over the dish and refrigerate for up to 6 hours. Do not deep-freeze.

Garnish the dish with a few crisp lettuce leaves and sprinkle paprika over the pears shortly before serving. Serve with thin brown bread and butter.

Mushroom Cocktail

☆   ①   ◫ ◫   ⧗

Preparation and cooking time:
30 minutes
Serving time: *about 10 minutes*
SERVES 4

½ lb. button mushrooms
5 fl. oz. water
salt
1 teaspoon butter
4 tablespoons mayonnaise (see page 63)
3 tablespoons double [heavy] **cream**
2 teaspoons horseradish sauce
few drops of Worcestershire sauce
1 teaspoon lemon juice
black pepper
heart of 1 small lettuce
To garnish:
cucumber slices

Wash the mushrooms, and halve or quarter any large ones. Put them into a saucepan with the water, a pinch of salt and the butter. Cover, bring to the boil, and simmer for about 10 minutes.

Remove the mushrooms from the liquid and chill them. Cook the mushroom liquid in an open pan until it is reduced to about 1 tablespoon. Blend together the mayonnaise, cream, cooled mushroom liquid, horseradish sauce, Worcestershire sauce and lemon juice. Season to taste with salt and pepper.

Refrigerate the mushrooms and dressing separately for up to 2 days. The dressing cannot be deep frozen because it contains mayonnaise.

Shred the lettuce finely and put in the base of four glasses. Blend the mushrooms and dressing together, spoon into the glasses, and garnish with the cucumber slices.

Florida Cocktail

☆   ①   ◫   ⧗

Preparation time: *15 minutes*
Serving time: *minimal*
SERVES 4

1 large grapefruit
3 large oranges
1 lime
sugar (optional)
To decorate:
1 small lime, sliced (optional)

Peel the grapefruit and oranges and remove the segments (see the easy hint on this page). Squeeze the juice from the lime and add to the juice in the bowl together with the fruit segments. Mix well, add sugar if necessary, and arrange in four individual small glasses

Refrigerate for up to 8 hours. Do not deep freeze.

Decorate each glass with a slice of lime before serving, if these are used.

Savoury Stuffed Courgettes

☆   ①   ◫ ◫   ⧗

Preparation and cooking time:
1 hour 10 minutes
Serving time: *about 30 minutes*
SERVES 4

4 medium-to-large courgettes [zucchini]

12

salt
1 tablespoon oil
1 small onion, finely chopped
1 slice bacon, de-rinded and
    chopped
¼ lb. mushrooms, chopped
3 tomatoes, chopped and peeled
1 tablespoon chopped parsley
1 clove of garlic, crushed
pepper

Cook the whole unpeeled courgettes in boiling salted water for 10 minutes. Drain. When they are cool enough to handle, cut them in half, scoop out the seeds, and chop the flesh roughly. *Heat* the oil in a pan, and fry the onion and bacon for about 5 minutes until golden. Add the mushrooms, and cook for a further 5 minutes. Stir in the tomatoes, chopped courgettes, parsley, garlic and seasoning, cover, and simmer gently for 20 minutes. Spoon the tomato mixture back into the courgette cases and place in a greased ovenproof dish.

The covered dish may be stored at room temperature for up to 6 hours, refrigerated for up to 1-2 days, or deep-frozen.

Heat oven to 375°F (Gas Mark 5, 190°C).
Bake, uncovered for 30 minutes. Serve piping hot.

Globe Artichokes with Curry Mayonnaise

☆   ① ①   ◻   ◼

Preparation and cooking time:
55 minutes
Serving time: *minimal*
SERVES 4

4 globe artichokes
salt
½ pint [1¼ cups] mayonnaise (see
    page 63)
2 teaspoons mild curry powder
a squeeze of lemon juice
1 tablespoon mango chutney, finely
    chopped

Wash the artichokes well in cold water and trim off any stalks to the base. Cook the artichokes in boiling salted water for 45 minutes or until a leaf can be pulled out easily. Drain and allow to cool. Blend the mayonnaise with the

curry powder, lemon juice and chutney.

The artichokes can be left at room temperature for up to 12 hours, or refrigerated for up to 2 days. The mayonnaise sauce will keep in a covered container in the refrigerator for a week. Do not deep freeze either the sauce or the artichokes.

Serve the artichokes on individual plates and hand the sauce around separately.

Jamaican Grapefruit

☆   ① ①   ◻   ◼

Preparation time: *about 10 minutes*
Serving time: *minimal*
SERVES 4

2 large grapefruit
3 tablespoons brown sugar
3 tablespoons rum
To decorate:
4 glacé cherries

Cut the grapefruit in half. Remove all the segments and put into a bowl. Sprinkle with the brown sugar and rum, and mix well. Pile the mixture back into the grapefruit skins.

Refrigerate the mixture for up to 6 hours, but do not deep-freeze.

Decorate each grapefruit half with a glacé cherry just before serving.

Chilled Melon and Pineapple

☆   ①   ◻   ◼

Preparation time: *20 minutes*
Serving time: *minimal*
SERVES 6

1 small pineapple or 1 lb. canned
    pineapple pieces or cubes
1 small to medium-sized melon
1 tablespoon chopped fresh mint
1 tablespoon lemon juice
sugar
To decorate:
mint sprigs (optional)

Cut the fresh pineapple into slices. Peel, remove the core, cut the flesh into pieces and put into a bowl. Drain the canned pineapple well. Cut a slice off the top of the melon and remove the seeds. Scoop out the flesh, using either a Parisienne cutter to make balls, or a spoon. Put the melon flesh into the bowl with the pineapple, together with any melon juice. Mix well and add the mint, lemon juice and sugar to taste. Pile the pineapple and melon back into the melon skin.

Cover the melon and keep at room temperature for up to 6 hours, but chill for 1½ hours before serving. Do not deep-freeze.

Decorate the melon with the sprigs of mint before serving, if these are used.

French Bean and Egg Salad

☆   ①   ◻   ◼

Preparation and cooking time:
about 30 minutes
Serving time: *minimal*
SERVES 4

½ lb. fresh or frozen French beans
salt
1 clove of garlic, crushed
4 tablespoons French dressing
    (see page 63)
2 hard-boiled eggs
2 tomatoes, quartered
pepper
1 tablespoon chopped chives
    (optional)

Cook the beans in boiling salted water for about 8 minutes; if frozen beans are used, follow the instructions on the packet. Drain. Mix the garlic with the French dressing, and toss the beans in this while they are still warm. Allow to cool.
Shell and quarter the eggs and add them to the salad with the tomatoes and seasoning. Turn the salad into a serving dish and sprinkle with the chives, if these are used.

Store the salad, covered, at room temperature for up to 6 hours, or refrigerate for up to 24 hours. Do not deep-freeze.

Serve the salad with brown bread and butter.

13

PÂTÉS

Melba Toast

Melba toast is traditionally served with pâté and some soups, and is not difficult to make. Put slices of white bread, about ¼ inch thick, under the grill [broiler], and toast both sides until golden brown. Remove from the grill and cool slightly. Cut off the crusts, then slice each piece of toast in two through the soft crumb part, so that you produce two squares each with one side untoasted. With the untoasted side uppermost, replace under a medium grill until it is golden (do not use too hot a grill or it will burn).

Melba toast keeps for weeks in an airtight container.

Creamy Kipper Pâté

☆ ① ⧖ ⧖

Preparation and cooking time:
35 minutes
Serving time: *minimal*
SERVES 4-6

1 lb. kipper fillets
1 small clove of garlic, crushed
6 tablespoons olive oil
3 tablespoons single [light] **cream**
salt and pepper
To garnish:
lemon slices

Poach the kippers in water for 10 minutes until they are just cooked. Drain and remove the skins, then put the cooked flesh into a saucepan and beat with a wooden spoon to break it up. Beat in the garlic and heat gently, stirring to prevent it from sticking. Add the olive oil gradually, beating well between each addition. Beat in the cream. Remove from the heat and season. Turn into a serving dish.

Cover and refrigerate for up to 2-3 days, or deep-freeze.

Garnish the pâté with lemon slices and serve with Melba toast or thin brown bread and butter.

Hare or Rabbit Terrine

☆ ☆ ① ① ⧖ ⧖ ⧖

Preparation and cooking time: *3¼ hours*
Serving time: *minimal*
SERVES 12

1 small hare or 1 large rabbit (about 3 lb), skinned
½ lb. lean pork
¾ lb. fatty bacon, de-rinded
1 large onion
1 tablespoon chopped parsley
1 teaspoon chopped fresh thyme (or ¼ teaspoon dried)
1-2 cloves of garlic, crushed
salt and freshly milled black pepper
4 tablespoons red wine
2 tablespoons brandy (optional)
4 slices streaky bacon, de-rinded

Heat oven to 325 °F (Gas mark 3, 170 °C).

Bone the hare or rabbit and cut the back meat carefully into strips. Put this on one side and mince [grind] the pork, bacon and onion. Add the parsley, thyme, garlic, seasoning, wine and brandy, and mix together until well-blended. Place half the mixture in the bottom of a large, well-greased terrine or earthenware casserole. Lay the reserved strips of meat from the back of the hare and the bacon slices on top, and cover with the remaining minced mixture. Cover the dish with foil and then a lid. Stand the dish in a roasting tin containing 1-inch of cold water.
Bake for 2½ hours. Remove from the oven, take off the lid and place weight on top of the foil.

Refrigerate for at least 6 hours before serving. It can be kept refrigerated for up to 5 days, or deep-frozen.

Serve sliced, with hot toast or French bread and butter.

Note: The bones from the hare, on which quite a bit of meat will remain, can be used to make a delicious soup.

Chicken Liver and Bacon Pâté

☆ ① ⧖ ⧖ ⧖

Preparation and cooking time:
1 hour 40 minutes
Serving time: *minimal*
SERVES 4-6

¼ lb. chicken liver
¼ lb. fatty bacon, de-rinded
1 small onion, chopped
1 clove of garlic, crushed
2½ oz. [5 tablespoons] butter
5 fl. oz. milk
1 blade mace (or a good pinch of ground mace)
1 bay leaf
2-3 peppercorns
½ oz. [2 tablespoons] flour
½ teaspoon anchovy essence
1 teaspoon prepared mustard
salt and pepper
To seal:
2 oz. butter, melted

Heat oven to 350 °F (Gas mark 4, 180 °C).
Gently fry the liver, bacon, onion and garlic in 2 ounces [4 tablespoons] of the butter for about 10 minutes. Remove from the heat, and either purée in a blender or mince [grind]. Put the milk into a saucepan with the mace, bay leaf and peppercorns. Bring slowly to the boil, remove from the heat, and leave for 5 minutes. Melt the remaining butter in a saucepan, add the flour and cook for 1 minute.
Gradually add the strained milk and bring to the boil, stirring all the time until it thickens. Remove from the heat and stir in the meat mixture, anchovy essence and mustard. Season to taste. Turn into a small, well-greased terrine and cover with a lid or foil. Stand in a roasting tin containing 1-inch of cold water and bake in a moderate oven for 1 hour. Allow to cool, then spoon the melted butter over it.

Refrigerate for up to 3-4 days or deep-freeze.

Serve from the terrine with hot toast and butter.

Aubergine Pâté

☆ ☆ ① ① ⧖ ⧖ ⧖

Preparation and cooking time:
1 hour 35 minutes
Serving time: *minimal*
SERVES 4-6

2 large aubergines [eggplants]
4 tablespoons olive oil
juice of 1 lemon
1 clove of garlic, crushed
salt and pepper
To garnish:
onion rings

Heat oven to 350 °F (Gas Mark 4, 180 °C).
Lightly score the aubergine skins. Put the aubergines on a baking tray, and bake in for 1¼ hours or until they are completely soft. When they are cool enough to handle, cut in half and scoop out the pulp. Put this into a bowl and pound or mash until it is fairly smooth. Beat in the oil gradually, then add the lemon juice, crushed garlic, and seasoning to taste.

Cover and refrigerate for up to 3-4 days, or deep-freeze.

Garnish with onion rings, and serve with hot toast or French bread and butter.

---

opposite: Chicken Liver and Bacon Pâté, Aubergine Pâté

FISH FIRST COURSES

The Use of Herbs in Fish Cookery

Most fish has a rather delicate flavour and it is important that the right herbs are used fairly sparingly, so that their flavour does not overpower that of the fish. Strongly flavoured herbs, such as sage, are not frequently used. The best herbs to use with fish are bay leaves – only in very small quantities; chives – excellent in fish salads or for sprinkling on cold dishes; dill – good with most fish: the dried herb is particularly good; fennel – both the feathery top and the bulbous stem can be used; tarragon – the chopped leaves should be used sparingly.

below: Devilled Crab
right: Scampi Provençale
opposite: Haricot Bean Salad with Tuna

Devilled Crab

Preparation time: *20 minutes*
Serving time: *minimal*
S E R V E S 4

1 medium-sized crab or ½ lb. canned
  crab meat
5 tablespoons mayonnaise (page 63)
2 teaspoons prepared mustard
¼–½ teaspoon Tabasco sauce
2 sticks celery, chopped
2 spring onions [scallions], chopped
salt and pepper
4 large lettuce leaves
To garnish:
chopped spring onions [scallions]

If a fresh crab is used, remove all the meat from the body and large claws. Drain canned crab meat well. Put the meat into a bowl and add the mayonnaise, mustard, Tabasco, celery and onions. Season to taste.

Cover and refrigerate for up to 8 hours. Do not deep-freeze.

Put the lettuce leaves on 4 small plates or scallop shells. Spoon the crab mixture on top and garnish with the onions.

Scampi Provençale

Preparation and cooking time:
35 minutes
Serving time: *about 5-10 minutes*
S E R V E S 4

1 oz. [2 tablespoons] butter, or 2
  tablespoons olive oil
1 medium-sized onion, chopped
1 clove or garlic, crushed
1 lb. tomatoes
1 tablespoon dry sherry
1 tablespoon chopped parsley
salt and pepper
½ lb. cooked scampi [shrimp]
To garnish:
1 tablespoon chopped parsley

Heat the butter or oil in a pan. Add the onion and garlic and cook gently for about 10 minutes or until the onion is soft. Peel the tomatoes, cut into quarters and remove the seeds. Add to the pan with the parsley, sherry and seasoning. Cover and cook for 10 minutes.

Refrigerate in a covered container for up to 3-4 days, or deep-freeze.

Reheat the sauce gently, stir in the scampi, and simmer gently for about 5 minutes or until piping hot. Serve sprinkled with the chopped parsley.

Savoury Fish with Cheese

☆   ① ①   ⋈   ⋈

Preparation time: *15 minutes*
Serving time: *about 25 minutes*
SERVES 4

4 small fillets plaice, sole or flounder
salt and pepper
1 small shallot, very finely chopped
    (or 1 tablespoon very finely
    chopped onion)
1½ teaspoon chopped fresh dill (or
    ½ teaspoon dried dill)
5 fl. oz. single [light] cream
1 oz. [¼ cup] Cheddar cheese,
    grated
1 oz. [⅓ cup] fresh white breadcrumbs

Season the fish with salt and pepper, fold in half or roll up, and either put each into a ramekin dish, or all into one large dish. Add the onion, dill and seasoning to the cream and pour over the fish.

Cover the fish tightly and refrigerate for up to 8 hours. Do not deep-freeze.

Heat oven to 375 °F (Gas Mark 5, 190 °C).
Sprinkle the fish with the cheese and breadcrumbs mixed together. Bake for 20 minutes.

Haricot Bean Salad with Tuna

☆   ①   ⋈ ⋈ ⋈

Preparation and cooking time:
2 hours, plus overnight soak for the beans
Serving time: *minimal*
SERVES 4

½ lb. haricot beans [dried white beans]
1 pint [2½ cups] stock, or water and
    1 chicken stock cube
1 sprig tarragon (or a good pinch of
    dried tarragon)
4 tablespoons French dressing
    (see page 63)
1 clove of garlic, peeled
½ lb. canned tuna
1 tablespoon chopped parsley
¼ small onion, very finely chopped
To garnish:
1 tomato, thinly sliced
1 sprig of parsley

Soak the haricot beans in cold water overnight. Drain. Put into a saucepan with the stock, tarragon and garlic. Cover, bring to the boil, and simmer gently for 1½ hours or until the beans are tender. Drain, and remove the tarragon sprig and garlic. Toss the beans while still warm in the French dressing and oil from the can of tuna, and add the parsley and onions. Season well with salt and pepper and allow to cool. Flake the tuna and mix with the beans. Turn into a serving dish.

Cover the salad and store at room temperature for up to 6 hours, or refrigerate for up to 2 days. Do not deep-freeze.

Garnish the salad with slices of tomato and the sprig of parsley shortly before serving.

SOUPS

Croûtons

Croûtons of fried bread are delicious served with most soups. It is better not to use very fresh bread, as this is difficult to cut into squares. Remove the crusts from slices of bread, about $\frac{1}{4}$-inch thick, then cut the bread into $\frac{1}{2}$-inch squares. Fry these in deep or shallow fat until golden brown; cooking in deep fat produces a more even colour. Remove the croûtons from the pan and drain on absorbent paper. For garlic croûtons, sprinkle with garlic salt immediately after frying.

Chilled Summer Soup

☆ ① ▨ ▨ ▣

Preparation and cooking time:
50 minutes
Serving time: *minimal*
SERVES 4-6

1½ oz. [3 tablespoons] **butter**
½ **lettuce, chopped**
1 bunch **watercress, chopped**
1 bunch **spring onions [scallions],**
  chopped
¾ pint [2 cups] **milk**
¾ pint [2 cups] **water**
1 chicken **stock cube**
salt and pepper
5 fl. oz. **yogurt**

Heat the butter in a pan. Add the
lettuce, watercress and spring onions,
and cook in a covered pan over a gentle
heat for 10 minutes. Add the water,
milk, stock cube and seasoning, bring
to the boil and simmer for 20 minutes
or until the vegetables are tender.
Remove from the heat, and either sieve
or purée in a blender. Add the yogurt
and whisk well.

Chill the soup in a soup tureen or other
suitable container. It can be refrigerated
for up to 2-3 days, or deep frozen.

Serve very cold with Melba toast (see
page 10).

Lentil Soup with Bacon

☆ ① ▨ ▨ ▣

Preparation and cooking time:
*1 hour 25 minutes, plus 2 hours soaking
time for lentils*
Serving time: *about 30 minutes*
SERVES 4-6

2 pints [5 cups] **stock, preferably**
  bacon stock, or use water and
  stock cubes (2 chicken and 1 beef)
6 oz. [1 cup] **lentils**
1 oz. [2 tablespoons] **butter or**
  margarine
2 onions, **chopped**
2 carrots, **chopped**
salt and pepper

---

opposite: Iced Avocado Soup
above: Lentil Soup, Artichoke Soup

5 fl. oz. single [light] **cream**
3 slices streaky **bacon, de-rinded**

Put the lentils to soak in the cold stock,
for 2 hours or longer. Melt the butter or
margarine in a saucepan and fry the
onions and carrots for about 5 minutes.
Stir in the stock and lentils, cover and
simmer gently for 1 hour. Sieve the
soup or purée in a blender. Season.

The soup can be kept at room
temperature for a few hours, or can be
refrigerated for up to 3 days. It deep-
freezes very well. As this soup is
especially good if made with bacon
stock, it is a good idea to make it after
boiling a bacon joint and then to
deep-freeze it.

Re-heat the soup gently and stir in the
cream just before serving. Do not
allow the soup to boil after the cream
has been added. Chop the bacon into
½-inch pieces. Fry until crisp and
sprinkle over the soup just before
serving.
Serve with croûtons.

Iced Avocado Soup

☆ ① ① ▨ ▨ ▣

Preparation time: *about 10 minutes*
Serving time: *minimal*
SERVES 4

2 ripe **avocados**
juice of ½ a **lemon**
½ pint [1¼ cups] canned **consommé**
5 fl. oz. sour **cream** or fresh single
  [light] **cream**
salt and pepper

Cut the avocados in half and cut 4 slices
for decoration. Dip these in lemon juice
to preserve the colour. Remove the
stones from the avocados and scoop out
the flesh. Sieve the flesh and mix with
the remaining ingredients, or purée all
the ingredients in a blender. Mix well,
taste, and adjust the seasoning.

Turn into a soup tureen and chill. This
soup should not be made more than
about 4 hours before it is required, as it
tends to discolour. It does not deep-
freeze well. If the top of the soup
changes colour, whisk well just before
serving.

Serve in a soup tureen with a few ice
cubes floating on the top.

Artichoke Soup

☆ ① ▨ ▨ ▣

Preparation and cooking time: *1 hour*
Serving time: *about 15 minutes*
SERVES 4

1 lb. Jerusalem **artichokes**
1 oz. [2 tablespoons] **butter or**
  margarine
1 onion, **chopped**
4 sticks **celery, chopped**
1 pint [2½ cups] **stock, or water and**
  1 chicken stock cube
½ pint [1¼ cups] **milk**
½ oz. [2 tablespoons] **cornflour**
  [cornstarch]
salt and pepper
To garnish:
1 tablespoon chopped **parsley**

Peel the artichokes under cold running
water to prevent discolouration. Chop
roughly. Melt the butter in a pan and
sauté the artichokes, onion and celery
gently in a covered pan for about 10
minutes. Add the stock, cover, and
simmer gently for about 35 minutes or
until the vegetables are very soft.
Either rub the soup through a sieve or
purée in a blender. Gradually blend the
milk into the cornflour. Heat the soup
to boiling point, then add the milk and
continue to cook, stirring all the time
until the soup has thickened. Taste,
and adjust the seasoning.

Remove from the heat and allow to cool.
The soup can be stored at room
temperature for up to 6 hours, or
refrigerated for up to 3-4 days. It
deep-freezes very well.

Reheat the soup gently until piping hot.
Sprinkle with parsley and serve with
croûtons.

19

top: Cassoulet
from left to right in front: raw
ingredients for Spring Lamb Casserole,
Chicken Marengo, Kidneys with
Red Wine

MAIN COURSES

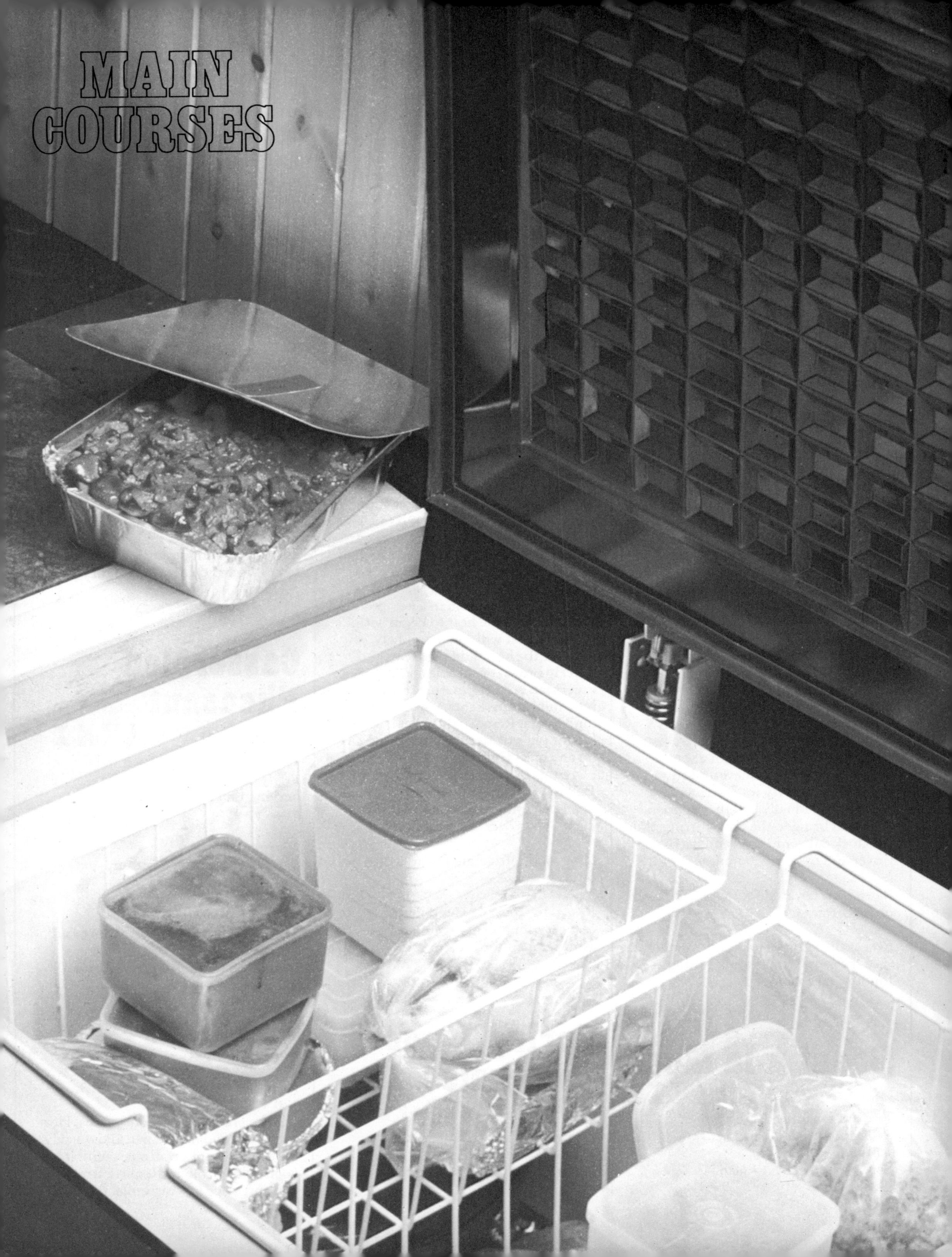

CASSEROLES & STEWS

Kidneys with Red Wine

☆ ① ⊠ ⊠

Preparation and cooking time:
55 minutes
Serving time: *about 40 minutes*
SERVES 4

4 large pig kidneys or 16 lamb
    kidneys
1 oz. [4 tablespoons] **flour**
salt and pepper
1 oz. [2 tablespoons] **butter or
    margarine**
1 large onion, chopped
5 fl. oz. water
½ pint [1¼ cups] **red wine**
1 beef stock cube
2 teaspoons French mustard
pinch of mixed dried herbs

Heat oven to 350 °F (Gas Mark 4,
180 °C).
Skin the kidneys and remove the cores.
Cut the pig kidneys into ½-inch pieces
or halve the lamb kidneys; toss in the
flour seasoned with salt and pepper.
Melt the butter or margarine in a pan
and fry the onion gently for about 5
minutes. Add the kidneys and any
excess flour and fry for a further 5
minutes. Gradually add the water and
wine and bring to the boil, stirring. Add
the stock cube, mustard and herbs.
Cover and cook for 30 minutes.

Refrigerate covered for up to 1-2 days,
or deep-freeze.

Reheat the kidneys for about 40 minutes
(use the same temperature setting as
for original cooking).

Boeuf à la Mode

☆ ☆ ① ① ⊠ ⊠ ⊠ ⊠ ⊠

Preparation and cooking time:
*3¼ hours, plus at least 12 hours to
marinate*
Serving time: *about 1 hour*
SERVES 6-8

3-4 lb. rolled topside [top round] **of
    beef**
2 large carrots, sliced
1 large onion, chopped
1-2 cloves garlic, crushed
1 bouquet garni
6 peppercorns
1 teaspoon mixed spice
1 pint [2½ cups] **red wine**
½ lb. fatty bacon, cut in 1-inch cubes
2 pints [5 cups] beef stock, or water
    and 2 stock cubes
1 calf's foot, cleaned and skinned,
    or 1 pig's trotter

Put the meat into a large bowl with the
carrots, onion, garlic, bouquet garni,
peppercorns, mixed spice and red wine.
Leave for at least 12 hours turning from
time to time. Remove the meat from
the marinade and dry.
Heat oven to 325 °F (Gas Mark 3,
170 °C). Fry the bacon in a heatproof
dish over a gentle heat to begin with,
so that the fat will run out. Then
increase the heat, add the meat, and
quickly brown on all sides. Pour off any
excess fat. Add the marinade and the
remaining ingredients. Cover and cook
for 3 hours. Remove the meat and calf's
foot or pig's trotter from the dish. Take
off any meat from the foot, chop, and
place this in a casserole with the beef.
Boil the remaining liquid rapidly in an
open pan until reduced to 1¼ pints [3
cups]. Pour over the meat.

Cover and refrigerate for up to 2-3 days,
or deep-freeze.

Reheat the meat, covered, in the
casserole for about 50 minutes (use the
same temperature setting as for original
cooking).

Spring Lamb Casserole

☆ ① ⊠ ⊠ ⊠

Preparation and cooking time:
1 hour 35 minutes
Serving time: *about 30 minutes*
SERVES 4

1½ lb. lean boneless lamb
1 oz. [2 tablespoons] **butter or
    margarine**
1 oz. [4 tablespoons] **flour**
1 pint [2½ cups] water
2 leeks, sliced in rings
1 lb. small young carrots, cleaned
1 chicken stock cube
¼ lb. mushrooms, sliced
4 oz. [1 cup] fresh or frozen peas

Heat oven to 350 °F (Gas Mark 4,
180 °C).
Cut the lamb into 1½-inch cubes. Heat
the butter or margarine in a pan and fry
the meat on all sides for about 5
minutes. Stir in the flour and cook,
stirring for about 2 minutes.
Gradually add the water, and bring to
the boil. Turn into a casserole with the
leeks, carrots and stock cube. Cover and
cook for 1½ hours; adding the
mushrooms and peas for the last 15
minutes.

Refrigerate, covered, for up to 2-3 days,
or deep-freeze.

Reheat the casserole for about 30
minutes or until piping hot (use the
same temperature setting as for original
cooking).

Casseroled Pheasant

☆ ☆ ① ① ① ⊠ ⊠ ⊠ ⊠

Preparation and cooking time:
2¼-4½ hours
Serving time: *about 45 minutes*
SERVES 4

1 large pheasant
1 oz. [2 tablespoons] **butter**
1 tablespoon oil
1 large onion, sliced
2 oz. [½ cup] **flour**
1 pint [2½ cups] stock, or water and
a stock cube
grated zest and juice of 1 orange
1 tablespoon red currant jelly
5 fl. oz. port
1 bay leaf
1 sprig of parsley
salt and pepper

Heat oven to 325 °F (Gas Mark 3,
170 °C).
Cut the pheasant into four pieces. Heat
the butter and oil in a pan and quickly
fry the pheasant on all sides until it is a
good golden colour. Remove from the
pan and place in a casserole. Add the

onion to the pan and cook until soft. Mix in the flour and cook, stirring for a few minutes until golden brown. Gradually add the stock and bring to the boil, stirring all the time. Allow to thicken and add the remaining ingredients. Pour over the pheasant, cover, and cook for 2-4 hours, depending on the age of the bird.

Refrigerate, covered, for up to 2-3 days, or deep-freeze.

Reheat the casserole for 45 minutes (use the same temperature setting as for original cooking).

Beef Goulash

Preparation and cooking time:
1 hour 50 minutes
Serving time: *about 30 minutes*
SERVES 4

1½ lb. good quality stewing beef
seasoned flour
1 oz. [2 tablespoons] **dripping**
1 large onion, chopped
1½ tablespoons paprika
1 lb. canned tomatoes
5 fl. oz. beef stock, or water and a
   stock cube
salt and pepper
5 fl. oz. sour cream, or double
   [heavy] cream mixed with 1
   tablespoon lemon juice

Cut the meat into 1½-inch cubes and toss in seasoned flour. Heat the dripping gently in a pan and fry the onion for a few minutes. Add the meat and paprika and cook, stirring, for a further 5 minutes until the meat is evenly browned. Add the canned tomatoes and the stock and bring to the boil, stirring all the time. Cover the pan and simmer gently for 1½ hours or until the meat is tender. Taste and adjust the seasoning.

Refrigerate, covered, for up to 2-3 days or deep-freeze.

Reheat gently, stirring occasionally. Stir in the cream, but do not boil again.

Cassoulet

Preparation and cooking time:
4 hours 10 minutes, plus overnight soak for the beans
Serving time: *about 1 hour*

SERVES 4-6

1 lb. haricot beans [dried white beans]
2¼ pints [5½ cups] **stock, or water and
   2 stock cubes**
½ lb. pickled pork [salt pork]
½ lb. stewing lamb (without bone)
1 oz. [2 tablespoons] **lard or dripping**
1 large onion, chopped
2 cloves of garlic, crushed
¼ lb. lean bacon
4 tablespoons concentrated tomato
   purée
1 bay leaf
1 teaspoon mixed dried herbs
½ lb. garlic sausage
2 oz. [⅔ cup] **white breadcrumbs**

Soak the beans overnight in cold water. Drain and put into a saucepan with the stock. Cover and simmer for 1½ hours, or until the beans are tender. Soak the pork for 2-3 hours in cold water, drain. *Heat* oven to 325°F (Gas Mark 3, 170°C). Cut the pork and lamb into 1-inch cubes. Melt the lard or dripping in a heatproof dish and fry the onion, garlic, pork, lamb and bacon for about 10 minutes. Add the beans, together with the stock, tomato purée, bay leaf, herbs and garlic sausage. Mix well. Cover and cook for about 2 hours.

Refrigerate, covered, for up to 4 days, or deep-freeze.

Sprinkle the top of the cassoulet with the breadcrumbs and reheat, uncovered, for 1 hour (use the same temperature setting as for original cooking).

Hot Madras Curry

Preparation and cooking time:
2 hours 40 minutes
Serving time: *about 50 minutes*
SERVES 4

1½ lb. chuck steak
2 tablespoons oil
1 onion, chopped
1 green pepper, chopped
1 tablespoon Madras curry powder
1 tablespoon curry paste
2-3 pieces dried whole ginger
5 fl. oz. water
salt

Heat oven to 325°F (Gas Mark 3, 170°C).

Cut the beef into 1½-inch cubes. Fry the beef in the oil with the onion, pepper, curry powder and paste for about 10 minutes, stirring. Add the ginger, water and salt, and transfer to a casserole. Cook for 2 hours, and then remove the ginger.

Refrigerate covered for up to 3-4 days, or deep-freeze.

Reheat the curry in a warm oven for 50 minutes (use the same temperature setting as for original cooking).

Chicken Marengo

Preparation and cooking time:
1 hour 50 minutes
Serving time: *about 50 minutes*
SERVES 4

4 chicken pieces
2 oz. [4 tablespoons] **butter**
2 tablespoons olive oil
4 shallots or 2 medium-sized onions,
   chopped
1 oz. [4 tablespoons] **flour**
4 tablespoons concentrated tomato
   purée
5 fl. oz. dry sherry
¾ pint [1¼ cups] **chicken stock**
½ lb. mushrooms
bouquet garni
pinch of sugar
salt and pepper

Dry the chicken pieces well. Heat half of the butter and the oil in a pan and fry the chicken on all sides for about 10 minutes until golden brown. Remove from the pan. Add the shallots or onions and cook gently for 5 minutes. Stir in the flour and cook for a minute. Add the tomato purée, then the sherry and stock. Bring to the boil, stirring all the time. Return the chicken to the pan with the mushroom stalks, bouquet garni, sugar and seasoning. Cover and simmer very gently for 1 hour. Remove the chicken from the pan and place in a casserole. Strain the sauce over.

Refrigerate, covered, for up to 2-3 days, or deep-freeze.

Heat oven to 350°F (Gas Mark 4, 180°C). Cook the casserole for about 40 minutes. Fry the mushrooms in the remaining butter and use to garnish.

SAVOURY PIES & PUDDINGS

Pastry Decorations

The most usual decoration is the pastry leaf, made by cutting out small diamonds of pastry, and marking on veins with a knife.

Equally simple, but slightly less usual, are crescents. These are made with a plain or fluted circle cutter, using only part to cut small crescents. The top of a small bottle or jar could also be utilised.

Simple lattices over a pie or flan always look effective: if you use a pastry wheel they can look particularly elegant.

If the filling of a pie looks interesting, cut a cross in the centre of the pie and pull the pastry edges back on themselves to expose the filling.

Chicken and Sweetcorn Pie

☆　　①　☒ ☒　☒

Preparation and cooking time: 1¼ hours
Serving time: *about 40 minutes*
SERVES 4

2 large chicken legs
½ pint [1¼ cups] water
sprig of thyme (or a good pinch of
　dried thyme)
a squeeze of lemon juice
salt and pepper
1½ oz. [3 tablespoons] butter
1½ oz. [⅓ cup] flour
5 fl. oz. milk
11 oz. [1½ cups] canned sweet corn,
　drained
8 oz. short crust pastry (see page 61)

Put the chicken legs into a saucepan with water, thyme, lemon juice and seasoning. Bring to the boil, cover and simmer gently for 40 minutes. When the joints are cool enough to handle, remove from the stock, take the meat off the bone and chop. Use the butter, flour, and milk, and the stock from cooking the chicken, to make a sauce (see page 63). Add the corn together with the chicken. Turn into a pie dish. Make up the pastry and cover the pie dish (see page 61).

Refrigerate, covered, for up to 24 hours, or deep-freeze.

Heat oven to 400°F (Gas Mark 6, 200°C). Bake the pie for 40 minutes until golden brown.

Steak and Kidney Pudding

☆　　①　☒ ☒ ☒ ☒

Preparation and cooking time:
4½ hours
Serving time: *about 1 hour*
SERVES 4

8 oz. suet crust pastry (see page 62)
1¼ lb. stewing beef
¼ lb. ox kidney
1 oz. [4 tablespoons] flour
salt and pepper
1 onion, chopped
water

Make up the pastry and line a 2½ pint [6 cup] greased pudding bowl (see page 61). Cut the beef into 1-inch cubes and the kidney into ½-inch pieces. Toss the meat in the flour seasoned with salt and pepper. Put the steak, kidney and onion in alternate layers in the bowl. Pour in enough water to come to within 1-inch of the top of the bowl. Roll out the remaining pastry to a circle the size of the top of the bowl. Moisten the edges and press firmly on the top to seal. *Cover* the bowl with a double layer of greased greaseproof [waxed] paper or foil, with a 1-inch pleat in the centre to allow for the pudding to rise. Steam for 4 hours.

Renew the covers and refrigerate for up to 2-3 days, or deep-freeze.

Steam the pudding for 1 hour before serving.

Beef and Pepper Pie

☆ ☆　　①　☒ ☒　☒

Preparation and cooking time: *2 hours*
Serving time: *about 30 minutes*
SERVES 4

1½ lb. stewing beef
1 oz. [4 tablespoons] flour
salt and pepper
1 oz. [2 tablespoons] lard or dripping
1 onion, chopped
2 green peppers, chopped
1 pint stock [2½ cups], or water and a
　stock cube
4 oz. quick rough puff pastry (see
　page 62)

Cut the beef into 1½-inch cubes. Toss in the flour seasoned with salt and pepper. Melt the lard or dripping in a pan and fry the onion, peppers and meat on all sides for about 5 minutes. Add the stock and bring to the boil. Cover and simmer gently for 1½ hours. Turn the meat and most of the gravy into a pie dish (the remainder of the gravy can be served with the pie). Make up the pastry and cover the pie (see page 62).

Refrigerate, covered, for up to 24 hours or deep-freeze.

Heat oven to 425°F (Gas Mark 7, 220°C). Bake the pie for about 30 minutes until golden brown.

Veal and Ham Pie

☆ ☆ ☆ ① ①　☒ ☒ ☒ ☒

Preparation and cooking time:
3 hours 10 minutes
Serving time: *minimal*
SERVES 4-6

1 lb. stewing veal
½ lb. lean bacon
1 tablespoon chopped parsley
¼ teaspoon grated nutmeg
salt and pepper
12 oz. hot water crust pastry (see
　page 62)
2 hard-boiled eggs
beaten egg to glaze
2 teaspoons powdered gelatine
5 fl. oz. stock

Heat oven to 400°F (Gas Mark 6, 200°C). *Chop* the veal and bacon, then blend in

24

the parsley, nutmeg and seasoning. Make up the pastry (see page 62). Using two-thirds of the pastry, mould it around the inside of a 6-inch diameter loose-bottomed cake tin. Put half the filling into the tin, then the eggs, and then the remaining filling.

Pat the rest of the pastry out to a circle for the lid. Place this on top and pinch the edges together to seal, trimming off any excess pastry. Make a slit in the top of the pie for the steam to escape.

Bake the pie for 10 minutes, then lower the heat to warm (325°F, Gas Mark 3, 170°C) and cook for a further 2¼ hours. Half-way through cooking, remove the pie from the cake tin and brush all over with beaten egg.

Allow the baked pie to cool. Soften the gelatine in the stock, then put in a bowl over a pan of gently simmering water until dissolved. Allow to cool, but not to set. Carefully pour the cool gelatine mixture through the hole in the top.

Refrigerate for up to 3 days, or omit the eggs and deep-freeze.

Serve cut in wedges like a cake.

above: Veal and Ham Pie
right: Beef and Pepper Pie

SAVOURY FLANS

*opposite clockwise from top left:
Quiche Lorraine, Salmon Flan with
Cucumber, Pissaladière, Cheese and
Leek Flan*

Salmon Flan with Cucumber

☆☆ ① ◔◔ ◆

Preparation and cooking time:
1 hour 20 minutes (including flan case)
Serving time: *about 20 minutes*
SERVES 4-6

½ lb. canned salmon
2 egg yolks
½ pint [1¼ cups] single [light] cream
   or milk
2 inch piece cucumber
¼ teaspoon anchovy essence
3 spring onions [scallions] chopped
salt and freshly milled black pepper
1 baked 8-inch deep flan case (see
   page 61)
To garnish:
sliced cucumber

Heat oven to 350°F (Gas Mark 4,
180°C).
Put the drained salmon into a bowl and
flake. Beat in the egg yolks, then the
cream. Peel and dice the cucumber, and
add to the fish together with the
anchovy essence, spring onions and
seasoning. Spoon the fish mixture into
the flan case, and bake for 30 minutes
or until the egg mixture is just set.

Store for up to 8 hours at room
temperature, or refrigerate for up to
2-3 days. Do not deep-freeze.

Serve the flan cold, or reheat in oven
for about 20 minutes (use the same
temperature setting as for original
cooking). Serve garnished with the
sliced cucumber.

Pissaladière

☆☆ ① ◔ ◆◆

Preparation and cooking time:
50 minutes (including flan case)
Serving time: *about 1 hour*
SERVES 4

4 tablespoons olive oil
2 large onions, chopped
1 lb. tomatoes, peeled and chopped
1 tablespoon concentrated tomato
   purée
1-2 cloves of garlic, crushed
1 teaspoon fresh chopped rosemary
   (or ¼ teaspoon dried rosemary)
salt and freshly milled black pepper
1 baked 8-inch deep flan case (see
   page 61)
2 tablespoons grated Parmesan
   cheese
1 small can anchovies
black olives

Heat the oil in a saucepan and fry the
onions over a gentle heat for about 10
minutes. Add the tomatoes, tomato
purée, garlic, rosemary and seasoning.
Cover and simmer for about 20 minutes,
then cook in an open pan for about 10
minutes, stirring until thick.

Store at room temperature for several
hours or refrigerate for up to 4 days. It
will deep-freeze.

Heat oven to 350°F (Gas Mark 4,
180°C).
Sprinkle the base of the flan case with
the Parmesan cheese and spoon over
the tomato mixture. Cut the anchovy
fillets in half lengthways and arrange in
a lattice over the top of the flan. Brush
all over the top of the tomato mixture
with oil from the anchovy can. Arrange
olives in the squares of the lattice. Bake
the flan for about 30 minutes or until
piping hot.

Quiche Lorraine

☆☆ ① ◔◔ ◆

Preparation and cooking time:
1 hour 40 minutes (including flan case)
Serving time: *about 20 minutes*
SERVES 4-6

1 baked 9-inch shallow flan case
   (see page 61)
¼lb. Emmenthal [Swiss] cheese,
   thinly sliced
4 slices streaky bacon, de-rinded
   and halved
2 eggs
5 fl. oz. milk or single [light] cream
1 teaspoon chopped parsley
1 teaspoon chopped chives
salt and pepper
To garnish:
4 tomatoes, sliced

Heat oven to 350°F (Gas Mark 4,
180°C).

Lay the slices of cheese in the bottom of
the flan case and top with the bacon.
Beat the eggs, the milk or cream, and
the herbs and seasoning together. Pour
into the flan case.
Bake for about 30 minutes or until the
egg mixture is just set.

Store for up to 8 hours at room
temperature, or refrigerate for up to
2-3 days. It will deep-freeze.

Serve the Quiche cold, or reheat in a
moderate oven for about 20 minutes.
(Use the same temperature setting as
for original cooking.) Garnish with the
sliced tomato.

Cheese and Leek Flan

☆☆ ① ◔◔ ◆

Preparation and cooking time:
1 hour 20 minutes (including flan case)
Serving time: *about 25 minutes*
SERVES 4

1 lb. leeks, sliced in rings
½ pint [1¼ cups] water
salt
1½ oz. [3 tablespoons] butter
1½ oz. [⅓ cup] flour
½ pint [1¼ cups] milk
6 oz. [1½ cups] grated Cheddar cheese
pepper
1 baked 8-inch deep flan case (see
   page 61)
To garnish:
parsley sprigs

Cook the leeks in the boiling salted
water for about 10 minutes or until they
are just tender.
Make up a white sauce with the butter,
flour and milk (see page 63). Add the
leeks and the water in which they were
cooked to the sauce, and mix well.
Remove from the heat, stir in nearly all
of the cheese, and season to taste.

Refrigerate the sauce in a covered
container for up to 3-4 days, or
deep-freeze.

Heat oven to 400°F (Gas Mark 6,
200°C). Reheat the flan case in a fairly
hot oven for 10 minutes. Reheat the
sauce over a gentle heat, stirring from
time to time until piping hot. Pour into
the flan case and sprinkle with the
remaining cheese. Put under a
pre-heated grill [broiler] until brown.
Serve garnished with the parsley sprigs.

27

ROASTS

Interesting Gravy

A well-flavoured gravy can turn a good roast dish into a superb one. In these recipes the bones are removed from the meat before roasting; simmer these in water with an onion, carrot and a few herbs to provide stock. Gravy does not have to be made at the last minute; one or two tablespoons of fat from around the joint can be spooned off half way through cooking, and used to make the gravy. It is important to brown the flour slowly; this improves, not only the colour, but the flavour as well. For special roasts, add 1 or 2 tablespoons of sherry or port to the gravy.

Breast of Veal with Piquant Lemon Stuffing

☆ ☆   ①   ⊠   ✕✕

Preparation and cooking time:
40 minutes
Serving time: *about 2½ hours*
SERVES 6

4 lb. breast of veal
½ small onion, finely chopped
3 slices bacon, de-rinded and
    chopped
2 oz. [4 tablespoons] butter
4 oz. [1 cup] fresh white breadcrumbs
1 tablespoon chopped parsley
grated zest and juice of ½ a lemon
1 small cooking apple, peeled and
    grated
salt and pepper
1 egg, beaten
To garnish:
1 green eating apple, sliced

Bone the joint, or ask the butcher to do it for you. Fry the onion and bacon in the butter for 5 minutes, then mix with the remaining ingredients. Lay the meat skin side downwards and spread the stuffing over the meat. Roll up and tie in several places with string.

Refrigerate, loosely wrapped in foil, for up to 48 hours, or deep-freeze.

Heat oven to 350 °F (Gas Mark 4, 180 °C).
Place the meat, still wrapped in foil, in a roasting tin, and roast for 2½ hours. During the last 30 minutes of cooking time, remove the foil, baste well with the juices, and continue cooking uncovered. Serve garnished with the sliced apple (dipped in lemon juice to preserve the colour).

Shoulder of Lamb with Chestnut Stuffing

☆   ①   ⊠   ✕✕

Preparation time: *30 minutes*
Serving time: *about 1¾ hours*
SERVES 4-6

3 lb. shoulder of lamb
½ lb. canned unsweetened chestnut
    purée
½ small onion, finely chopped
¼ lb. pork sausagemeat
grated zest and juice of ½ a lemon
½ teaspoon fresh chopped rosemary
    (or ¼ teaspoon dried rosemary)
salt and pepper
1 small egg, beaten

Bone the shoulder, or ask the butcher to do it for you. Mash the chestnut purée, then add the remaining stuffing ingredients and mix together well.
Lay the meat flat on a board with the skin side down, and spread the stuffing evenly over the surface. Roll the meat up and secure with string.

Refrigerate, loosely wrapped in foil or greaseproof [waxed] paper for up to 24 hours, or deep-freeze.

Heat oven to 425 °F (Gas Mark 7, 220 °C).
Roast the lamb for 20 minutes, then lower the heat to 375 °F (Gas Mark 5, 190 °C) and cook for a further hour.

Crunchy Pork with Nut Stuffing

☆   ①   ⊠   ✕✕

Preparation time:
40 minutes
Serving time: *about 2 hours*
SERVES 8

4 lb. loin of pork with the skin
4 oz. [1 cup] soft white breadcrumbs
1 onion, peeled and grated
1 stick celery, finely chopped
½ teaspoon grated nutmeg
2 oz. [½ cup] walnuts, chopped
1 oz. [¼ cup] seedless raisins
1 egg, beaten
salt and pepper

Bone the loin and score the skin, or ask the butcher to do this for you. Mix together all the remaining ingredients so that they are well blended. Lay the meat skin side downwards and press the stuffing against the meat, from where the bones were removed.

Refrigerate, loosely wrapped in foil, for up to 48 hours, or deep-freeze.

Heat oven to 425 °F (Gas Mark 7, 220 °C).
Unwrap the meat, place in a roasting tin, and roast for 20 minutes. Lower the heat to 375 °F (Gas Mark 5, 190 °C) and roast for a further 1 hour 40 minutes.

Boned and Roast Stuffed Duck with Oranges

☆ ☆ ☆ ① ①   ⊠ ⊠   ✕✕

Preparation time: *1 hour*
Serving time: *about 2 hours*
SERVES 8

5 lb. duck
1 lb. calf or lamb liver
1 lb. pork sausagemeat
1 tablespoon chopped parsley
1 clove garlic, crushed
1 tablespoon brandy (optional)
salt and pepper
3 medium-sized oranges
To garnish:
1 orange, thinly sliced

Place the duck, breast side down, on a wooden board. Using a very sharp, and fairly small knife, cut through the back skin down to the back bone, and then carefully work the flesh away from the carcass, pressing the knife against the carcass and taking all the meat away from the bone with the skin.

Remove the bones from the legs and wings by scraping the flesh away, but leave the drumstick bones in place. Mince the calf or lamb liver and mix with the sausagemeat, parsley, garlic and brandy if used. Season well with salt and pepper. Peel the oranges, removing all the white pith, then cut each orange in half lengthways. Open out the duck and remove any excess fat.

Spread half the liver mixture down the centre of the duck, then lay the orange halves along the stuffing with their cut sides uppermost. Spread the remaining stuffing over the oranges. Fold the ends of the duck in over the stuffing, then fold the sides into the centre to form a parcel. Sew the edges together with fine string or coarse thread.

Refrigerate, loosely covered with foil or greaseproof paper, for up to 24 hours, or deep-freeze.

Heat oven to 400 °F (Gas Mark 6, 200 °C).

Prick the skin of the duck all over with a fork. Roast uncovered for 20 minutes, then lower the temperature to 350 °F (Gas Mark 5, 180 °C) and roast for a further 1 hour 40 minutes. Serve garnished with the sliced orange.

below: Breast of Veal with Piquant Lemon Stuffing
right: Boned and Roast Stuffed Duck with Oranges

COLD DISHES

Green Salads

It is a good idea to vary both the ingredients and the dressing for these. Try using not only lettuce, watercress, cucumber and celery but also endive, green peppers, kohlrabi and Chinese cabbage. The salad should be well-tossed in French dressing so that every leaf is coated, but not so that it is swimming in dressing. Flavour the dressing with garlic, French mustard, chopped fresh herbs (parsley, chives, tarragon, basil, mint), or a few finely chopped capers or gherkins.

Rice Salad with Pork and Apricots

☆   ①   ⊠   ⊠

Preparation and cooking time:
30 minutes
Serving time: *minimal*
SERVES 4

¼ lb. dried apricots
8 oz. [1¼ cups] long-grain rice
salt
6 tablespoons French dressing (see page 63)
½ bunch spring onions [scallions] chopped
1 lb. cooked pork, thinly sliced
1 oz. [¼ cup] seedless raisins
2 oz. [½ cup] blanched almonds, toasted

Soak the apricots in cold water for about 6 hours. Drain and chop. Cook the rice in boiling salted water for about 12 minutes or until just tender. Drain, put into a bowl and mix in the dressing while the rice is still hot. Stir in the apricots, spring onions and raisins and cool.
Arrange the pork around the edge of a serving dish. Pile the rice into the centre and sprinkle with the almonds.

Refrigerate, covered in foil, for up to 8 hours. The rice salad on its own can be refrigerated, covered, for 3-4 days. Do not deep-freeze.

Serve with a mixed green salad.

Glazed Ham and Beef Galantine

☆ ☆   ①   ⊠ ⊠ ⊠

Preparation and cooking time: *2¾ hours*
Serving time: *minimal*
SERVES 6-8

1¼ lb. lean chuck beef
½ lb. lean gammon or ham
4 oz. [1 cup] fresh white breadcrumbs
1 tablespoon chopped parsley
½ teaspoon mixed dried herbs
salt and pepper
2 eggs
To glaze and garnish:
enough aspic-flavoured gelatine to set ¼ pint [⅔ cup]

1 hard-boiled egg, sliced
1 tomato, sliced

Heat oven to 325 °F (Gas Mark 3, 170 °C).
Mince the meat finely, then mix with the breadcrumbs, herbs and seasoning, and bind with the eggs. Turn into a well-greased 2-lb. loaf tin, cover with a double layer of foil, and stand in a roasting tin containing 1-inch of cold water. Bake for 2 hours.
Remove from the oven and place weights on the top to press down the meat. Cool, then chill.
Turn the galantine out on to a wire rack with a plate underneath to catch any drips. Spoon a little of the cold aspic all over the meat loaf and leave to set. Pour a little of the aspic into a saucer, dip the slices of egg and tomato into this, and arrange them attractively over the top of the loaf: leave to set. Spoon the remaining aspic over the loaf.

Refrigerate for up to 24 hours; the unglazed loaf can be refrigerated for up to 2-3 days, or deep-frozen.

Serve the galantine cut in slices.

Terrine of Chicken with Lemon

☆ ☆   ① ①   ⊠ ⊠ ⊠ ⊠

Preparation and cooking time:
3 hours 20 minutes
Serving time: *minimal*
SERVES 8

3-4 lb. chicken
½ lb. fatty pork
2 onions
2 cloves garlic, crushed
2 tablespoons chopped parsley
½ teaspoon mixed dried herbs
grated zest and juice of 1 lemon
1 egg, beaten
salt and freshly milled black pepper

Heat oven to 325 °F (Gas Mark 3, 170 °C).
Remove the breast meat from the chicken and cut into neat strips. Take the rest of the chicken meat off the bones and mince [grind] with the pork and onions. Put into a bowl and add the remaining ingredients. Mix well. Put half the minced mixture into a well-greased terrine. Lay the strips of chicken breast on top and then cover

with the remaining chicken and pork mixture. Cover the terrine with foil and a lid. Stand in a roasting tin containing 1-inch of cold water and cook for 2½ hours. Remove from the oven and place weights on top of the chicken to press.

Refrigerate for up to 3-4 days or deep-freeze.

Turn out of the dish and serve.

Smoked Haddock Mousse

☆ ☆   ① ①   ⊠   ⊠

Preparation and cooking time:
40 minutes
Serving time: *minimal*
SERVES 6-8

1 lb. smoked haddock
½ pint [1¼ cups] water
enough aspic-flavoured gelatine to set ½ pint [1¼ cups]
2 eggs, separated
grated zest and juice of ½ a lemon
1 tablespoon dry sherry
½ teaspoon anchovy essence
5 fl. oz. double [heavy] cream, lightly whipped
To garnish:
sliced cucumber

Poach the haddock in the water for 10 minutes or until just cooked. Remove the fish from the pan, take off the skin and flake the fish finely. Using the liquid from poaching the fish, make up the aspic to ½ pint [1¼ cups], following the instructions on the packet. Beat the egg yolks with the lemon zest and juice, sherry and anchovy essence. Beat in the cooled aspic, then stir in the flaked fish. Put on one side and allow to stiffen slightly. Lightly whip the cream and fold into the jellied mixture. Whisk the egg whites stiffly and fold in. Turn the mixture into a lightly oiled 7-inch cake tin.

Refrigerate, covered, until set, or up to 2 days. It will deep-freeze.

Turn the mousse out and garnish with the cucumber.

---

*opposite: from left to right top row:
Smoked Haddock Mousse, Terrine of Chicken with Lemon, Glazed Ham and Beef Galantine
foreground: Rice Salad with Pork and Apricots*

FISH DISHES

Garnishes

These should not be fussy, nor take a great deal of time to make. Some of the best for fish are parsley (in sprigs or chopped), watercress sprigs, paprika (particularly good for adding colour to a pale dish), chopped chives, celery or fennel leaves, sliced or quartered tomatoes or lemons, and slices of cucumber and green pepper. Very often a little of one of the ingredients from a dish can be reserved to garnish it (as in the Sole Normandie). The art of garnishing is to make the dish look attractive without making its appearance over-elaborate.

below left: Stuffed Whole Baked Sea Bass
below right: Kulibyaka
opposite: Sole Normandie with Prawns

Kulibyaka, or Russian Fish Pie

Preparation and cooking time: *1 hour*
Serving time: *about 30 minutes*
SERVES 4

8 oz. quick rough puff pastry (see page 62)
2 oz. [⅓ cup] rice
salt and pepper
1 small onion, finely chopped
2 oz. [½ cup] mushrooms, finely chopped
2 oz. [4 tablespoons] butter
1 tablespoon chopped parsley
½ lb. canned salmon, drained and flaked
2 hard-boiled eggs, sliced

Make up the pastry (see page 62). Cook the rice in boiling salted water for 12 minutes and drain. Fry the onion and mushrooms in half the butter for 5 minutes. Roll out the pastry and cut into two rectangles, 12 inches x 6 inches. Lay one piece of pastry on a baking sheet. Put the ingredients in layers in the centre of the pastry: first the rice,

sprinkled with the parsley, then the onion and mushrooms, the salmon, and finally the egg slices. Season each layer lightly with salt and pepper. Damp the pastry edges and lay the second piece of pastry over the filling. Seal the edges.

Refrigerate, covered, for up to 24 hours. Do not deep-freeze.

Heat oven to 425°F (Gas Mark 7, 220°C).
Make four slits in the pastry for the steam to escape, and then bake for 30 minutes. Melt the remaining butter and pour into the escape holes.

Trawlers' Pie

Preparation and cooking time:
45 minutes
Serving time: *about 30 minutes*
SERVES 4

¾ lb. fresh cod fillet
¾ lb. smoked cod fillet
1 bay leaf
¾ pint [2 cups] milk
1½ oz. [3 tablespoons] butter

1½ oz. [⅓ cup] **flour**
2 teaspoons **anchovy essence**
1 teaspoon **Worcestershire sauce**
salt and pepper
¼ **lb. instant mashed potato mix**
3 oz. [¾ cup] **grated Cheddar cheese**

Put all the fish into a saucepan with the bay leaf and milk. Cover and poach for about 10 minutes. Remove the fish, skin and flake. Make up a white sauce using the butter and flour, and the milk from cooking the fish (see page 63). Stir the fish, anchovy essence, Worcestershire sauce and seasoning into the white sauce and turn into an ovenproof dish. Make up the potato following the instructions on the packet, but use a little extra liquid so that the potato spreads easily. Spread over the fish mixture.

Cover and refrigerate for up to 24 hours, or deep-freeze.

Heat oven to 400°F (Gas Mark 6, 200°C).
Sprinkle the cheese over the potato and bake for about 30 minutes.

Stuffed Whole Baked Sea Bass

✩　　　① ①　　🞨　　　🞨 🞨

Preparation and cooking time:
40 minutes
Serving time: *45 minutes—1 hour*
SERVES 6-8

4-5 **lb. sea bass, bream, or red**
　　snapper, cleaned
salt and pepper
3 **onions**
2 **sticks celery, chopped**
4 oz. [½ cup] **butter**
5 oz. [1¼ cups] **fresh white**
　　breadcrumbs
¼ **lb. canned crab meat**
1 **egg, beaten**
1 **chicken stock cube**
½ pint [1¼ cups] **water**

Sprinkle the fish with salt and pepper inside and out. Finely chop 1 onion and fry in half the butter with the celery until soft. Stir in the breadcrumbs, drained and flaked crab meat and egg, and stuff the cavity of the fish. Secure the opening with string latticed between cocktail sticks [tooth picks].

Refrigerate wrapped in foil for up to 24 hours, or deep-freeze.

Heat oven to 350°F (Gas Mark 4, 180°C).
Unwrap the fish and place in a large baking tin. Dissolve the stock cube in the water and pour into the tin. Melt the remaining butter and brush over the fish. Top with the remaining onions, cut into rings. Bake uncovered for 45 minutes to 1 hour.

Sole Normandie with Prawns

✩ ✩ ✩ ① ① ① 🞨 🞨　　🞨

Preparation and cooking time: *1 hour*
Serving time: *about 30 minutes*
SERVES 4

1 **lb. prawns or shrimps**
2 **large or 4 small sole, filleted**
bouquet garni
salt and pepper
¾ pint [2 cups] **water**
5 fl. oz. **white wine**
¼ **lb. button mushrooms**
1½ oz. [3 tablespoons] **butter**
1½ oz. [⅓ cup] **flour**
5 fl. oz. **single [light] cream**

To garnish:
parsley sprigs

Shell most of the prawns, reserving a few for garnishing. Put the shells, the fish bones, the bouquet garni and seasoning into a large saucepan. Add the water and bring slowly to the boil. Simmer for about 10 minutes. Strain off into another pan, and add the wine.
Roll the fillets of fish up and poach each in the stock, removing them with a draining spoon and placing in an ovenproof dish. Then simmer the sliced mushrooms in the stock. Make a sauce with the butter, flour and fish stock (see page 63). Stir in the shelled prawns, taste, and adjust the seasoning.

Refrigerate the fish, tightly wrapped in foil, and the sauce, covered with foil, for up to 8 hours. Do not deep-freeze.

Heat oven to 350°F (Gas Mark 4, 180°C).
Keep the fish covered and reheat in the oven for 20 minutes. Reheat the sauce very gently, stirring from time to time, and add the cream with any liquid from the fish. Pour the sauce over the fish and garnish with the reserved prawns and parsley.

DESSERTS

PIES FLANS & GATEAUX

Quick Gâteaux

The cake base for a gâteau could be a plain sponge mix or a bought one. Fresh fruit gâteaux can be quickly made by adding fruit in season, and whipped fresh cream. To give extra flavour to a plain cake base, sprinkle with a little brandy, rum, kirsch, or other liqueur. Fresh whipped cream or butter cream can also be flavoured with a little liqueur. Nuts make a very good addition to the filling, and can of course be used for coating the sides, or for sprinkling on the top.

Sponge Flan Cases

These are always popular, and are particularly good when filled with fresh fruit. They do not store as well as pastry flan cases, but may be kept in an airtight tin for up to 2 days, or may be deep-frozen. To make an 8-in. case, whisk 2 eggs and 2 ounces [4 tablespoons fine] castor sugar in a bowl, over a pan of gently simmering water, until the mixture is thick. Remove the bowl from the heat and fold in 2 ounces [½ cup] of sieved self raising flour (or plain flour sieved with ½ teaspoon of baking powder). Turn the mixture into a greased and floured flan mould, and bake in a fairly hot oven for 25 minutes. Turn out, and allow to cool.

from left to right: top shelf: Normandy Apple Flan, Coffee Soaked Gâteau, Lemon Meringue Pie
bottom shelf: Fresh Strawberry Layer Gâteau, Chocolate Rum Gâteau, Bakewell Tart, Orange Cream Flan
foreground: Gâteau Diane

Fresh Strawberry Layer Gâteau

☆ ☆　①①　⧖　⧗

Preparation and cooking time:
50 minutes
Serving time: *about 15 minutes*
SERVES 8-10

**4 egg Victoria sandwich cake
   mixture (see page 62) using 3 oz.
   [½ cup] ground almonds in place
   of 3 oz. [¾ cup] of the flour
1 lb. fresh strawberries
½-1 pint [1¼-2½ cups] double [heavy]
   cream, lightly whipped
extra sugar
1 oz. [¼ cup] flaked browned almonds**

Heat oven to 375°F (Gas Mark 5,
190°C).
Make the cake mixture (see page 62)
and divide it between 3 prepared 8-inch
sandwich tins. Bake for 20 minutes,
then turn out of the tins and cool on
a rack.

Store the cake-base in an airtight tin for
up to 2-3 days. Keep the finished
gâteau in a cool place for up to 6 hours.

Cut almost all the strawberries in half,
reserving a few for the top. Spread
one-third of the cream over one of the
cake layers. Top with half the prepared
strawberries, sprinkle with sugar, and
add another cake layer. Repeat the
cream and strawberry layers, and top
with the remaining cake. Spread the
rest of the cream over the top, and
decorate with the whole strawberries
and flaked almonds.

Chocolate Rum Gâteau

☆ ☆ ☆ ①①　⧖ ⧖　⧗

Preparation and cooking time: *1½ hours*
Serving time: *about 30 minutes*
SERVES 8-10

**4 eggs
¼ lb. [½ cup] castor [fine] sugar
3 oz. [¾ cup] self-raising flour, or
   plain [all-purpose] flour sifted with
   ¼ teaspoon baking powder
1 oz. [¼ cup] cocoa
3 tablespoons oil**

**5 oz. [½ cup] butter
9 oz. [2 cups] sifted icing
   [confectioners'] sugar
5 tablespoons rum
6 tablespoons evaporated milk
½ lb. plain [semi-sweet] chocolate
To decorate:
crystallized ginger**

Heat oven to 350°F (Gas Mark 4,
180°C).
Whisk the eggs and sugar until the
whisk leaves a trail when lifted out of
the mixture. Sift the flour and cocoa
together and fold into the mixture, then
fold in the oil. Turn into a prepared
8-inch cake tin and bake for 45 minutes.
Turn out and cool on a rack, then cut
the cake into 4 rounds.

Store the cake-base in an airtight tin for
up to 3 days. Store the completed
gâteau in a tin for up to 24 hours.

Cream the butter and gradually beat in
the icing [confectioners'] sugar, and 3
tablespoons of the rum. Spread this on
the bottom three layers of cake,
re-assemble it, and stand it on a rack.
Heat the evaporated milk and remaining
rum in a pan over a low heat until very
hot, but not boiling. Remove from the
heat and add the chocolate, broken up
into small pieces. Stir until the chocolate
has melted; if necessary return the pan
to a very gentle heat. Cool, stirring until
the icing coats the back of a wooden
spoon. Pour over the cake and leave to
set. Decorate with the crystallized
ginger.

Coffee Soaked Gâteau

☆　①①　⧖ ⧖　⧗

Preparation and cooking time:
1 hour 40 minutes
Serving time: *minimal*
SERVES 8-10

**3 egg Victoria sandwich cake
   mixture (see page 62)
½ lb. [1 cup] sugar
¾ pint [2 cups] water
2 tablespoons brandy or Tia Maria
3 tablespoons coffee essence
½ pint [1¼ cups] double [heavy] cream
To decorate:
walnut halves**

Heat oven to 375°F (Gas Mark 5,
190°C).
Make the cake mixture (see page 62)

and turn it into a prepared 8-inch tin.
Bake for 45-50 minutes. Dissolve the
sugar in the water over a low heat.
Remove from the heat and add the
brandy or Tia Maria and coffee essence.
Turn the cake out of the cake tin and
stand on a serving plate. Pierce it all
over with a skewer then pour over the
hot coffee syrup.

Leave to stand for at least 12 hours.
Store covered with foil for up to 2 days,
or deep-freeze.

Cover the cake with the whipped cream
and decorate with the walnuts.

Gâteau Diane

☆ ☆　①①　⧖ ⧖ ⧖ ⧗

Preparation and cooking time: *5 hours*
Serving time: *about 1 hour*
SERVES 8-10

**6 eggs, separated
¾ lb. [1½ cups] castor [fine] sugar
½ lb. plain [semi-sweet] chocolate
12 oz. [1½ cups] unsalted butter
6 oz. [¾ cup] sugar
8 fl. oz. [1 cup] water
1 lb. canned pineapple pieces,
   drained
2 oz. [½ cup] flaked browned almonds**

Heat oven to 250°F (Gas Mark ¼,
130°C).
Mark out three 8-inch circles on
greased greaseproof [waxed] paper.
Whisk the egg whites stiffly, then
gradually whisk in half the castor sugar,
a teaspoon at a time. Fold in the
remaining castor sugar. Divide the
mixture between the three circles and
spread it right out to the edges. Bake
for about 4 hours or until the meringue
is hard.

Store the meringue base for up to 2
months, in an airtight tin. Store the
completed gâteau in a cake tin for up to
1-2 days, or deep-freeze.

Cream the butter. Melt the chocolate,
and beat it into the butter. Lightly beat
the egg yolks. Put the sugar and the
water into a pan over a gentle heat until
the sugar has dissolved, then boil
rapidly to 230°F or until the syrup
forms a long thread when dropped into
cold water. Gradually beat this into the
egg yolks, and then, slowly, into the
chocolate mixture. Spread one-third of
the chocolate icing, and half the
pineapple on to two rounds of

meringue. Pile one of these on top of the other, and add the third meringue. Spread the remaining chocolate icing over the top and sprinkle with the almonds.

Normandy Apple Flan

Preparation and cooking time:
1 hour 5 minutes
Serving time: *minimal*
SERVES 4-6

2 lb. cooking apples
3-4 tablespoons water
4 oz. [½ cup] sugar
6 oz. flan pastry (see page 61)
1 tablespoon lemon juice
2 tablespoons apricot jam, sieved

Heat oven to 375 °F (Gas Mark 5, 190 °C).
Peel, core and slice 1½ lb. of the apples. Put into a saucepan with the water and cook until very soft. Add the sugar and mash with a fork to a smooth purée. While the apples are cooking, make up the pastry, roll it out, and line an 8- or 9-inch flan ring (see page 61). Bake blind for 5 minutes. Remove the greaseproof [waxed] paper and beans and spoon in the apple purée. Peel and core the remaining apples and slice neatly. Arrange on top of the apple purée and brush with lemon juice. Bake for about 25 minutes or until the apples on top are cooked. Remove the flan from the oven and brush all over the top with warm, sieved apricot jam.

Refrigerate for up to 3 days, or deep-freeze.

Serve with fresh cream.

Orange Cream Flan

Preparation and cooking time:
40 minutes
Serving time: *minimal*
SERVES 4

4 oz. [1 cup] digestive biscuits [Graham crackers], crushed
2 oz. [4 tablespoons] butter

2 tablespoons brown sugar
juice of 3 oranges
½ oz. [2 tablespoons] cornflour [cornstarch]
1 tablespoon sugar
grated zest of 2 oranges
1 egg, separated
5 fl. oz. double [heavy] cream, lightly whipped
To decorate:
1 small orange, sliced

Crush the digestive biscuits with a rolling pin. Melt the butter in a saucepan, stir in the sugar and biscuit crumbs, and mix well. Press the mixture into an 8-inch flan ring or pie dish, to make a case, and chill while preparing the filling. Make the orange juice up to ½ pint [1¼ cups] with water. Blend the cornflour, sugar and orange zest with a little of the orange juice and heat the rest. When it boils, pour over the blended mixture, and stir well.
Return the mixture to the saucepan and bring to the boil, stirring all the time. Allow to thicken, then remove from the heat and beat in the egg yolk. Cover the sauce with a circle of damp greaseproof [waxed] paper and leave until cold.
Stiffly whisk the egg white. Fold first the cream and then the egg white into the sauce. Spoon into the biscuit crust case.

Refrigerate for up to 1-2 days, or deep-freeze.

Decorate the flan with slices of orange shortly before serving.

Lemon Meringue Pie

Preparation and cooking time:
1 hour 20 minutes (including flan case)
Serving time: *minimal*
SERVES 4-6

grated zest and juice of 2 large lemons
1½ oz. [6 tablespoons] cornflour [cornstarch]
½ pint [1¼ cups] water
2 egg yolks
8 oz. castor [1 cup fine] sugar
1 baked 8-inch flan case (see page 61)
3 egg whites

Heat oven to 350 °F (Gas Mark 4, 180 °C).
Blend the lemon zest and juice with the

cornflour in a basin. Bring the water to the boil and pour over the blended mixture, stirring. Return to the pan and bring to the boil, stirring all the time. Allow to thicken. Remove from the heat and stir in half of the sugar blended with the egg yolks. Cool slightly then spoon into the flan case. Whisk in half the remaining sugar, a teaspoon at a time. Fold in the last of the sugar. Spoon the meringue over the lemon filling, taking care to cover to the edge of the filling. Bake the pie for 15 minutes or until the meringue is golden.

Store at room temperature for up to 12 hours, or refrigerate for up to 2-3 days. Do not deep-freeze.

Serve cut into segments.

Bakewell Tart

Preparation and cooking time:
1 hour 20 minutes
Serving time: *minimal*
SERVES 4

4 oz. flan or short crust pastry (see page 61)
2 heaped tablespoons raspberry jam
2 oz. [4 tablespoons] butter
2 oz. [4 tablespoons] castor [fine] sugar
grated zest and juice of ½ a lemon
2 oz. [½ cup] cake crumbs
2 oz. [½ cup] ground almonds
2 eggs, beaten

Heat oven to 350 °F (Gas Mark 4, 180 °C).
Make up the pastry, roll out and use to line a 6-7-inch flan ring (see page 61). Spread the jam over the base of the flan. Cream the butter and sugar together until light and fluffy, then beat in the lemon zest and juice. Fold in the cake crumbs, ground almonds and beaten eggs, and spread the mixture on the jam. Roll out the pastry trimmings, and cut them into thin strips and use these to make a lattice over the top of the tart. Bake for 40 minutes or until the centre is firm.

Allow to cool, then store in an airtight tin for up to 2-3 days.

Serve with cream as a dessert.

HOT DESSERTS

Decorating Desserts

Pies with sweet fillings, which otherwise look a little plain, are usually improved by a sprinkling with sugar before serving – this adds a soft shine and makes them appear more appetizing. Plain mousses and creams may be topped with chopped nuts, grated chocolate, or a slice or twist of lemon or orange. And of course, if you have an icing bag, piped cream always looks impressively professional!!

Raspberry and Cream Stuffed Pancakes

☆　　ⅅ ⅅ　　⊠　　　Ⅺ

Preparation and cooking time:
30 minutes
Serving time: *about 20 minutes*
S E R V E S 4 - 6

½ pint [1¼ cups] pancake batter (see page 62)
½ lb. canned raspberries
5 fl. oz. sour cream, or double [heavy] cream mixed with 1 tablespoon lemon juice
1 tablespoon cornflour [cornstarch]

Make up 8-10 pancakes from the batter (see page 63). Drain the raspberries (reserve the syrup) and blend the raspberries with the cream. Place a little of this filling on each pancake, roll up, and place in an ovenproof dish.
Blend the cornflour with the raspberry juice in a saucepan and bring to the boil, stirring all the time. Boil for 1-2 minutes.

Cover the stuffed pancakes and refrigerate for up to 2 days, or deep-freeze. The sauce should be refrigerated or deep-frozen in a separate container.

Heat oven to 400°F (Gas Mark 6, 200°C).
Pour the sauce over the pancakes, cover and reheat for 20 minutes.

Apple Surprise Pie

☆　　　ⅅ　　⊠　　　Ⅺ

Preparation and cooking time:
55 minutes
Serving time: *about 25 minutes*
S E R V E S 4 - 6

½ pint [1¼ cups] water
6 oz. [¾ cup] sugar
peeled zest of ½ a lemon
a few cloves
2 lb. cooking apples
5 fl. oz. double [heavy] cream, lightly whipped
4 oz. short crust pastry (see page 61)
milk for glazing

Put the water into a saucepan with the sugar, lemon zest and cloves. Heat gently until the sugar has dissolved, then bring to simmering point. Peel, core and slice the apples; poach in the syrup for about 10 minutes.
Remove from the pan with a draining spoon, and place in a pie dish. Allow to cool, then spread the cream over the top. Make up the pastry and cover the top of the pie (see page 61).

Refrigerate, covered, for up to 2 days, or deep-freeze.

Heat oven to 400°F (Gas Mark 6, 200°C).
Brush the pastry with milk and bake for 25 minutes until just golden.

Upside Down Pudding

☆　　　ⅅ　　⊠ ⊠　　　Ⅺ

Preparation and cooking time: *1¾ hours*
Serving time: *about 30 minutes*
S E R V E S 6

2 oz. [4 tablespoons] butter
2 oz. [4 tablespoons] brown sugar
1 lb. canned pineapple rings
5-10 glacé cherries
5-10 walnuts
3 egg Victoria sandwich cake mixture (see page 62)

Heat oven to 350°F (Gas Mark 4, 180°C).
Melt the butter in an 8-inch cake tin over a very low heat. Sprinkle the sugar over, then arrange the well-drained pineapple rings, glacé cherries and walnuts attractively on top. Make up the cake mixture (see page 62) and spread evenly over the top of the fruit and nuts. Bake for 1¼ hours or until the top of the cake springs when lightly pressed.

Remove from the oven and cool in the tin. Store covered at room temperature for up to 2 days, or deep-freeze.

Keep the cake tin covered and reheat for 30 minutes (use the same temperature setting as for original cooking).

Crêpes Suzette

☆ ☆　　ⅅ　　⊠　　　Ⅺ

Preparation and cooking time:
30 minutes
Serving time: *about 10 minutes*
S E R V E S 4

½ pint [1¼ cups] rich pancake batter (see page 62)
3 oz. [6 tablespoons] unsalted butter
4 oz. [½ cup] sugar
2 teaspoons finely grated orange zest
juice of half an orange
2 tablespoons Cointreau or Curaçao
2 tablespoons brandy or rum
To decorate:
½ an orange, sliced

Make up 8-10 thin pancakes from the batter (see page 62).

Cover the pancakes and refrigerate for up to 1 week, or deep-freeze.

Heat the butter, sugar, orange zest and juice in a large frying pan or heatproof dish, over a gentle heat until the sugar has dissolved. Add the Cointreau or Curaçao. Fold each pancake into four. Put them into the pan and heat through gently in the sauce, turning twice. Decorate with the orange slices, pour on the brandy, and then flame the pancakes. Serve at once.

Note: It is best to use a long taper to light the brandy. Do not allow the sauce to heat for long after the brandy is added, or the flames may flare too high.

opposite: Crêpes Suzette

ICED DESSERTS

Pineapple Marshmallow Mousse

☆   ① ①   ⊠ ⊠ ⊠ ⊠

Preparation and cooking time: *30 minutes*
Serving time: *minimal*
SERVES 4-6

½ pint [1¼ cups] **unsweetened canned pineapple juice**
6 oz. [2 cups] **marshmallows (white or pink)**
juice of ½ a lemon
½ pint [1¼ cups] **double [heavy] cream**

Put the pineapple juice into a bowl with the marshmallows. Place the bowl over a pan of gently simmering water and cook, stirring from time to time, until the marshmallows have melted. Remove from the heat, add the lemon juice and cool.
Whip the cream fairly stiffly, then gradually beat in the pineapple and marshmallow mixture.

Turn into a suitable container and freeze. If deep-freezing, allow the mousse to soften in the refrigerator for about an hour before serving.

Serve scoops or spoonfuls of the mousse in individual dishes or glasses. This is delicious topped with a few slices of crystallized ginger.

Mocha Ice-Cream Charlotte

☆ ☆   ① ①   ⊠ ⊠ ⊠ ⊠

Preparation time: *40 minutes*
Serving time: *minimal*
SERVES 6-8

4 **eggs, separated**
4 oz. [1 cup] **sifted icing [confectioners'] sugar**
4 tablespoons **coffee essence**
½ pint [1¼ cups] **double [heavy] cream, lightly whipped**
1 lb. **plain [semi-sweet] chocolate finger biscuits [cookies]**

Whisk the egg whites until very stiff, then gradually whisk in the sugar. Beat the egg yolks with the coffee essence, then beat them gradually into the whisked whites. Carefully fold in the cream. Turn the mixture into an 8-inch cake tin; preferably one with a loose bottom.

Cover lightly with foil and freeze until firm. If deep-freezing, allow the ice cream to soften for 1 hour in the refrigerator before serving.

To serve the charlotte, turn the ice cream out of the cake tin and press the chocolate biscuits [cookies] round the sides. If you have difficulty in making them stick to the ice cream, run a hot knife quickly round the sides of the ice cream to melt it. Tie the biscuits in place with a ribbon.

Blackcurrant Sorbet

☆   ①   ⊠ ⊠ ⊠ ⊠

Preparation and cooking time: *30 minutes*
Serving time: *minimal*
SERVES 4

½ lb. **blackcurrants***
5 fl. oz. **water**
3 oz. [6 tablespoons] **sugar**
2 teaspoons **powdered gelatine**
1 **egg white**
*When fresh blackcurrants are not in season, use 1 pound canned black-currants, and omit the water and sugar.

Put the blackcurrants into a saucepan with the water. Cover and simmer them for about 10 minutes, or until they are tender. Remove from the heat and stir in the sugar. Soften the gelatine in 2 tablespoons of cold water, add to the hot blackcurrants, and stir until it dissolves completely. If canned blackcurrants are used, soften the gelatine in a bowl. Stand the bowl over a pan of gently simmering water and leave until dissolved, then stir into the blackcurrants.
Either sieve the blackcurrants or purée in a blender, then strain through a sieve to remove the pips. Turn into a suitable container and freeze. Stir once or twice. Whisk the egg white stiffly and fold into the blackcurrant mixture when it is thick, but not firm.

Freeze until firm. If deep-freezing, allow the sorbet to soften for about an hour in a refrigerator before serving.

Serve scoops of the sorbet in individual glasses. Top with a small cluster of fresh blackcurrants, when these are available.

Frozen Gooseberry Fool

☆   ① ①   ⧖ ⧖ ⧖ ⧖

Preparation and cooking time:
30 minutes
Serving time: *minimal*
SERVES 4

1 lb. gooseberries*
½ pint [1¼ cups] water
sprig of mint
4 oz. [½ cup] sugar
a little green colouring
½ pint [1¼ cups] double [heavy] cream, lightly whipped
To decorate:
mint sprigs, or a few reserved gooseberries
*When fresh gooseberries are not obtainable, use 1½ lb. canned gooseberries and omit the sugar and water. Drain off all but 6 tablespoons of the fruit syrup, then sieve or purée in a blender as below.

Top and tail the gooseberries. Put them in a pan with the water and mint, cover, and simmer gently for about 15 minutes until soft. Remove from the heat, stir in the sugar and a little green colouring. Discard the mint sprig. Sieve, or purée in a blender and then sieve to remove all the pips. Allow to cool, and blend the cooled mixture with the lightly whipped cream. Turn into 4 ramekin dishes.

Freeze until firm, then cover. If deep-freezing, allow the fool to soften in the refrigerator for 1 hour before serving.

Decorate each dish before serving.

top: *Frozen Gooseberry Fool*
right: *Mocha Ice-Cream Charlotte*

41

REFRIGERATOR DESSERTS

Sponge Finger Biscuits [Cookies]
These make an ideal accompaniment to refrigerated desserts. Whisk 2 large eggs with 2½ ounces [5 tablespoons] of castor [fine] sugar in a bowl, over a pan of gently simmering water, until the mixture is thick. Remove the bowl from the heat and carefully fold in 2 ounces [¼ cup] of plain [all-purpose] flour sifted with 1 tablespoon of cornflour [cornstarch]. Spoon the mixture into a piping bag fitted with a ½-in. plain pipe, and pipe out fingers onto a baking sheet covered with greaseproof [waxed] paper. Sprinkle with sugar, and bake in a hot oven for 8-10 minutes. Keep the biscuits attached to the paper, but turn them upside down on a working surface, and cover with a damp cloth until they loosen. Store in an airtight tin for 1-2 days.

Pineapple Ginger Cream

☆   ① ①   ▨ ▨ ▨

Preparation time: *20 minutes*
Serving time: *minimal*
SERVES 4

¾ lb. canned pineapple cubes
5 fl. oz. double [heavy] cream, lightly
   whipped
3 pieces stem ginger, finely chopped
1 tablespoon ginger syrup from the
   stem ginger jar
16 ginger biscuits [snaps]
To decorate:
slices of stem ginger

Drain the pineapple cubes and reserve the syrup. Cut each cube in half, then carefully fold them into the lightly whipped cream with the chopped ginger and syrup. Dip the biscuits in the pineapple syrup, then arrange round the sides of 4 small serving dishes. Spoon the cream mixture into the centre.

Refrigerate for at least 12 hours or up to 36 hours. Do not deep-freeze.

Decorate each portion with slices of ginger before serving.

Wine Posset

☆   ① ①   ▨ ▨   ▨

Preparation time: *15 minutes*
Serving time: *minimal*
SERVES 4

grated zest and juice of 1 large lemon
4 tablespoons white wine
2 oz. [4 tablespoons] castor [fine] sugar
½ pint [1¼ cups] double [heavy] cream
2 egg whites
To decorate:
½ lemon, thinly sliced

Place the grated lemon zest and juice, the wine and sugar into a bowl. Stir until the sugar has dissolved. Add the cream, then whisk the mixture until it forms soft peaks. Stiffly whisk the egg whites and fold into the mixture.

Turn into 4 glasses and refrigerate for up to 24 hours.

Decorate with a twist of lemon and serve with finger biscuits [cookies].

Uncooked Lemon Cheesecake

☆ ☆   ① ①   ▨ ▨   ▨

Preparation and cooking time:
50 minutes
Serving time: *minimal*
SERVES 6-8

grated zest and juice of 2 large
lemons
3 eggs, separated
4 oz. [½ cup] sugar
½ oz. [2 tablespoons] powdered
   gelatine
4 tablespoons water
5 fl. oz. single [light] cream
12 oz. [1½ cups] cottage cheese
5 fl. oz. double [heavy] cream, lightly
   whipped
4 oz. [1 cup] digestive biscuits
   [graham crackers], crushed
1 oz. [2 tablespoons] demerara [light
   brown] sugar
2 oz. [4 tablespoons] butter, melted
To decorate:
fresh fruit in season

Put the lemon zest and juice into a bowl with the egg yolks and white sugar. Stand the bowl over a pan of simmering water and whisk until thick and foamy. Remove the bowl from the heat and whisk until cool. Soften the gelatine with the water in a bowl, then stand over a pan of hot water until the gelatine has dissolved. Blend the single [light] cream into the cottage cheese, then carefully blend in the egg yolk mixture and gelatine. Put on one side until slightly thickened, but not set. *Whisk* the egg whites stiffly, then fold first the cream and then the egg whites into the cheese mixture. Turn into a lightly buttered 8-inch loose-bottomed cake tin and chill. Mix together the crushed biscuits, demerara sugar and melted butter and sprinkle this mixture over the set cheesecake. Press down lightly.

Refrigerate for up to 2 days, or deep-freeze.

Turn the cheesecake out of the tin on to a serving plate and decorate with fresh fruit in season.

Port Wine Jelly

☆ ☆   ① ①   ▨ ▨ ▨

Preparation and cooking time:
15 minutes
Serving time: *minimal*
SERVES 4

½ pint [1¼ cups] water
peeled zest and juice of 1 lemon
1-inch cinnamon stick
1 tablespoon red currant jelly
8 fl. oz. [1 cup] port wine
sugar

½ oz. [2 tablespoons] **powdered gelatine**

¼ **pint double** [heavy] **cream, lightly whipped**

1 oz. [¼ cup] **flaked browned almonds**

Put the water, the lemon zest, cinnamon stick and red currant jelly into a saucepan. Bring to the boil and simmer for 10 minutes. Add the port and lemon juice and sweeten to taste (the amount of sugar needed will depend on the kind of port used). *Heat* until just below boiling point. Meanwhile soften the gelatine in 3 tablespoons of cold water. Remove the port mixture from the heat and stir in the softened gelatine until it dissolves completely. Strain into a measure, and make up to 1 pint [2½ cups] with cold water if necessary. Pour the mixture into a glass dish.

Refrigerate for up to 2 days. Do not deep-freeze.

Spread the whipped cream over the top, sprinkle on the almonds, and serve well chilled.

below: Port Wine Jelly
top right: Wine Posset
bottom right: Pineapple Ginger Cream

PLANNED MEALS

FONDUE PARTY

left: Pavlova with Cherries
below: Fondue Bourguignonne with sauces

A meal of this sort can be great fun – a relaxing and informal way of entertaining your friends. But it is very important that care be taken with the hot fat required for cooking the meat, and a proper fondue pan is absolutely essential. If two pans are used, as we recommend, there is less danger of 'too many cooks' becoming impatient, and perhaps knocking the pan off the burner-stand. (Two pans will also mean that the oil will not reduce in heat too quickly; a problem which may occur when too much food is cooked at once.) Do also remember that the prongs of the special fondue forks become very hot, and these forks should not be put into the mouth.
A good wine to serve with this meal would be a dry red wine.

Cream of Celery Soup

Preparation and cooking time: *35 minutes*
Serving time: *about 15 minutes*
SERVES 8

1 large head of celery
2 pints [5 cups] stock, or water and
  stock cubes
1 bouquet garni
2 oz. [4 tablespoons] butter
2 oz. [½ cup] flour
1 pint [2½ cups] milk
5 fl. oz. single [light] cream
salt and pepper

Wash the celery carefully so that all the dirt is removed, then chop it finely. Bring the stock to the boil, add the celery and bouquet garni, cover the pan and cook gently for about 10 minutes or until the celery is just tender.
Meanwhile, melt the butter in a pan, add the flour and cook for 1 minute, stirring. Gradually stir in the milk, then the celery and stock and bring to the boil, stirring all the time. Remove from the heat and season to taste. Discard the bouquet garni.

Refrigerate, covered, for up to 2-3 days, or deep-freeze.

Reheat the soup gently and stir in the cream at the last moment. *Serve* with croûtons.

Fondue Bourguignonne

Preparation time: *1 hour*
Serving time: *minimal*
SERVES 8

3 lb. best rump steak or fillet steak
fondue sauces (see this page)
parsley
cooking oil

Cut the meat into 1-inch cubes and season very lightly with salt and pepper. Put into a bowl. Make up the sauces.

Refrigerate the meat and the sauces for up to 2 days. Do not deep-freeze.

Divide the meat among 8 dinner plates and garnish each one with a sprig of parsley or put on to one or two large plates. For 8 people it is better, if possible, to have two fondue pans, but one will be adequate. As the burners on most fondue pans are fairly slow, you will probably find it easier to heat the oil first on the stove and then carefully transport it to the table. Hand the sauces around separately.

Tartare Sauce

Blend ½ pint [1¼ cups] of mayonnaise with 2 tablespoons finely chopped gherkins, 1 tablespoon chopped parsley and 1 tablespoon chopped capers. Season well.

Sour Cream with Chives

Blend 5 fl. oz. sour cream with a finely crushed clove of garlic and 2 tablespoons chopped chives or spring onion [scallion] tops, and 2 tablespoons finely chopped watercress. Season with salt and pepper.

Cucumber and Yogurt Sauce

Peel and dice ¼ of a cucumber, put into a sieve, and sprinkle with 1 teaspoon of salt. Leave to drain for 15 minutes, then blend with 5 fl. oz. yogurt. Season with pepper, and more salt if necessary.

Sweet and Sour Tomato Sauce

Fry a medium-sized chopped onion in ½ oz. [1 tablespoon] butter or margarine for 5 minutes. Add 2 tablespoons tomato purée, 4 tablespoons

water, 2 tablespoons brown sugar, 2 tablespoons vinegar, 1 teaspoon Worcestershire sauce, 2 teaspoons prepared mustard, and seasoning. Bring to the boil and simmer for 5 minutes. Cool.

Horseradish Cream

Melt 1 tablespoon red currant jelly over a very low heat. Allow to cool, then carefully fold into 5 fl. oz. lightly whipped double [heavy] cream with 2 teaspoons of grated horseradish. Season to taste.

Pavlova

Preparation and cooking time:
4 hours 20 minutes, or less
Serving time: *about 10 minutes*
SERVES 8-10

5 egg whites
1½ teaspoons distilled malt vinegar
10 oz. [1¼ cups] castor [fine] sugar
2 teaspoons cornflour [cornstarch]
½ pint [1¼ cups] double [heavy] cream,
  lightly whipped
about 1½ lb. fresh prepared fruit
  (peaches, passion fruit pulp,
  raspberries, strawberries,
  cherries)

Heat oven to 250 °F (Gas Mark ¼, 130 °C).
Mark out a large circle, about 12-inches in diameter, on a piece of lightly oiled greaseproof [waxed] paper. Whisk the egg whites until stiff, then gradually whisk in the vinegar. Blend the sugar with the cornflour and gradually whisk in half the sugar, a teaspoon at a time. Fold in the remaining sugar.
Spread about half the meringue over the marked out circle, then put the remainder into a piping bag fitted with a large rose pipe. Pipe large swirls around the edge of the circle to make a flan case. Bake for 3-4 hours, or until firm to the touch. Remove carefully from the tray and cool.

Store the Pavlova in an airtight tin for up to 2-3 weeks.

Spread the cream over the inside of the meringue case and pile the fruit on top. Do not assemble the Pavlova more than about 2-3 hours before it is required or the fruit and cream will soften the case.

CELEBRATION DINNER

A special occasion calls for a really super menu – and enough pre-planning to allow the cook time to enjoy herself as much as her guests. Two of the three courses given here can be prepared an entire day in advance; the third can be finished, apart from last-minute touches, about 8 hours before serving.

If you want to serve wine with the meal, choose a light dry white, or a dry rosé. Sherry could be served with the Cornish Crab soup if you like, but be careful to choose a dry or medium-dry variety (the three tablespoons needed for the recipe can come from the same bottle).

Cornish Crab Soup

☆ ☆   ① ①   ⊠ ⊠   ⊠

Preparation and cooking time:
1 hour 10 minutes
Serving time: *about 20 minutes*
SERVES 6

1 medium-to-large crab (3-4 lb.), or 1
   small lobster (2-3 lb.)
1 pint [2½ cups] water
peeled zest of 1 lemon
juice of ½ a lemon
salt and pepper
1 bouquet garni
2 oz. [4 tablespoons] butter
1 onion, chopped
2 oz. [½ cup] mushrooms, sliced
½ pint [1¼ cups] single [light] cream

---

*opposite: from left to right on the sideboard: Stuffed Peaches in Brandy, Veal en Croûte
on the table: Cornish Crab Soup*

2 egg yolks
3 tablespoons dry sherry (optional)

Remove all the meat from the crab, or lobster. Put the well-scrubbed shell (including the claws) into a saucepan with the water, lemon zest and juice, seasoning and bouquet garni. Cover and simmer for 30 minutes.
Melt the butter in a pan and fry the onion and mushrooms gently for 10 minutes. Add the strained crab stock. Remove from the heat, allow to cool, and then add the crab meat.

Refrigerate, covered, for up to 8 hours, or deep-freeze.

Reheat the soup gently. Blend the cream with the egg yolks and sherry and add to the crab mixture. Heat without boiling. Serve with croûtons.

Veal en Croûte

☆ ☆   ① ①   ⊠ ⊠ ⊠ ⊠   ⊠

Preparation and cooking time:
2 hours 40 minutes
Serving time: *about 1 hour*
SERVES 6

3 lb. leg of veal, boned and rolled
salt and pepper
8 oz. canned liver pâté
3 tablespoons dry sherry
2 oz. [½ cup] mushrooms, finely
   chopped
1 small onion, finely chopped
14 oz. frozen puff pastry, defrosted

Heat oven to 350 °F (Gas Mark 4, 180 °C).
Season the meat with salt and pepper, wrap loosely in foil and roast for 2 hours. Allow to cool. Mash the liver pâté with the sherry, add the mushrooms and onion, mix well and

season to taste. Roll out the pastry to a rectangle, large enough to completely cover the meat. Trim the edges. Spread the mushroom mixture over the centre of the pastry, and place the meat on top. Dampen the pastry edges and bring them together to completely enclose the veal. Seal the edges well. Use the pastry trimmings to make leaves for decoration.

Refrigerate, covered, for up to 24 hours. Do not deep-freeze.

Heat oven to 425 °F (Gas Mark 7, 220 °C).
Place on a baking tray and bake for 30 minutes, then lower the heat to moderate (as previous setting) and bake for a further 30 minutes.

Stuffed Peaches in Brandy

☆   ① ① ① ⊠   ⊠

Preparation and cooking time:
55 minutes
Serving time: *minimal*
SERVES 6

½ pint [1¼ cups] water
4 oz. [½ cup] sugar
5 fl. oz. white wine
2 tablespoons brandy
6 large ripe peaches
1 oz. [2 tablespoons] blanched
   almonds, chopped
2 oz. [¼ cup] cut mixed peel [candied
   fruit]
5 fl. oz. double [heavy] cream, lightly
   whipped

Put the water, sugar, wine and brandy into a saucepan over a low heat until the sugar has dissolved. Peel the peaches (if they are difficult to peel, dip them in boiling water for 1 minute, and then peel). Gently poach the peaches in the brandy syrup for 15 minutes. Allow to cool.
Fold the peel and the almonds into the lightly whipped cream. Halve the peaches and remove the stones. Put a tablespoonful of the cream mixture on 6 halves, then sandwich the peaches together again. Arrange in a shallow serving dish, and pour over the syrup.

Refrigerate, covered, for up to 24 hours. Do not deep-freeze.

Serve with crisp biscuits [cookies].

47

INTIMATE DINNER

A dinner for two sometimes needs to be as out-of-the-ordinary as an elegant party for more people. And if you want to show you care a lot about a particular person – then what better way, than with this simple, yet super meal? It is a particularly easy one to prepare ahead of time, because all three courses can, if you need, be made and refrigerated up to 2 days in advance. This will give you lots of time to concentrate on table decorations, and the extra touches which can turn a good meal into a truly memorable one.

Perhaps it is your husband you want to surprise and impress – or an old and valued friend. Why not set a candle-lit table, with flowers and the very best cutlery and china – and a delicious accompanying wine, such as a full-bodied white Burgundy. And make sure good coffee and (if you like) a liqueur are available, to round off the meal.

Pimento Salad, or Peperonata

☆ ① ① ⊠ ⊠

Preparation and cooking time: 40 minutes
Serving time: minimal
SERVES 2

1 small onion, finely chopped
1 small clove of garlic, crushed
2 tablespoons olive oil
2 red peppers
salt and pepper

Cook the onion and garlic gently in the oil for 5 minutes. Cut the peppers into rings, discarding the core and seeds. Add them to the pan with the salt and pepper. Cover and cook gently for 25 minutes.

Refrigerate, covered, for up to 1-2 days, or deep freeze.

Serve chilled.

Savoury Veal Birds

☆ ☆ ① ① ⊠ ⊠ ⊠

Preparation and cooking time:
1 hour 50 minutes
Serving time: about 25 minutes
SERVES 2

2 large escalopes of veal
¼ lb. lean pork, minced [ground]
1 tablespoon finely chopped onion
1 tablespoon fresh white
  breadcrumbs
2 teaspoons chopped parsley
salt and pepper
2 slices streaky bacon, de-rinded
½ oz. [1 tablespoon] butter
1 tablespoon oil
2 carrots, chopped
1 onion, chopped
1 stick celery, chopped
1 level tablespoon flour
scant ½ pint [1¼ cups] white wine
1 bouquet garni
To garnish:
chopped parsley

Flatten out the veal escalopes, or ask the butcher to do so. Mix together the pork, finely chopped onion, bread-crumbs and parsley. Lay the escalopes out on a board and place half the pork mixture on each. Roll up tightly, turning in the sides of the meat to make a neat parcel. Stretch the slices of bacon with the back of a knife and wrap a bacon slice around each parcel. Secure the parcels with string. Heat the butter and the oil in a pan and gently fry the carrots, onion and celery for 5 minutes. Stir in the flour and cook for 1 minute. Gradually blend in the wine, then bring to the boil, stirring all the time. Add the veal rolls, bouquet garni and seasoning. Cover and simmer gently for 1 hour.

Refrigerate, covered, for up to 1-2 days, or deep-freeze.

Remove the string and the bacon from the veal rolls, and discard it. Reheat gently for about 20 minutes and serve sprinkled with chopped parsley.

Toffee-topped Grape Cream

☆ ① ① ⊠ ⊠ ⊠ ⊠

Preparation time:
15 minutes
Serving time: about 10 minutes
SERVES 2

¼ lb. grapes
5 fl. oz. double [heavy] cream
1 tablespoon brandy (optional)
2 teaspoons castor [fine] sugar
2 tablespoons demerara [light
  brown] sugar

Halve the grapes, remove the pips, and put most of the fruit into the bottom of a shallow ovenproof dish. Lightly whip the cream, then beat in the brandy and sugar. Spread this mixture over the grapes.

Refrigerate the dish for at least 6 hours, or up to 2 days. Do not deep-freeze.

Just before serving, sprinkle the demerara sugar over the cream and put under a pre-heated medium grill [broiler]. Grill for about 8 minutes, until the sugar melts and bubbles. Serve at once topped with a few reserved grapes. The contrast between the hot topping and the cold grapes is delicious.

opposite: Savoury Veal Birds, Toffee-topped Grape Cream, Pimento Salad

BUFFET PARTY

One of the easiest and most rewarding ways to entertain a large group of people is with a buffet party. The atmosphere is a relaxed and informal one, and allows guests to circulate and talk as they wish without the restrictions of table seating arrangements – which, in any case, few of us can readily arrange for large numbers. With this buffet menu you might like to serve mulled wine during the evening, and add French bread and a salad to the simple but satisfying Moussaka.

Mulled wine works best with a red: a Burgundy is ideal. To each litre [quart] bottle add 1 stick of cinnamon, ¼ teaspoon of ground ginger, the juice and peeled zest of a small lemon, a good sprig of fresh mint, and a liberal handful of cloves. Heat gently to simmering point, taste, and add sugar if necessary. Strain, and hand around in mugs. (For 12 people, 3 bottles should be ample.)

It is important that you supply enough plates, dishes and cutlery for all courses – borrow if necessary, rather than having to rush away and wash-up halfway through the evening. Paper napkins are essential – and since your guests may end up using their fingers for ease, finger bowls would make an extra thoughtful touch.

top: Moussaka
left: Savarin

Cold Stuffed Eggs with Mayonnaise

☆ ☆   ① ①   ⊠   ⊠

Preparation time: *20 minutes*
Serving time: *about 10 minutes*
SERVES 12

12 hard-boiled eggs
2 oz. [¼ cup] cooked ham, minced
few drops of Tabasco sauce
generous ½ pint [1¼ cups] mayonnaise
salt and pepper
2 oz. [¼ cup] shelled prawns [shrimps]
few drops anchovy essence
1 teaspoon horseradish sauce
milk
1 tablespoon tomato ketchup
To garnish:
watercress

Shell the eggs and cut in half lengthways. Put half the egg yolks into one bowl and the other half into a second bowl. Add the ham, Tabasco sauce, 2 tablespoons of the mayonnaise and the seasoning to one bowl. Mix well with the egg yolks and spoon back into the white cases. Place, cut side downwards, in a serving dish. Add the prawns, anchovy essence, 2 tablespoons of mayonnaise and seasoning to the remaining egg yolks, and mix as above. Place the stuffed eggs in a second serving dish.

Cover the eggs tightly and refrigerate for up to 8 hours. Do not deep-freeze.

Shortly before serving, mix the horseradish sauce and sufficient milk to give a coating consistency, with half the remaining mayonnaise. Spoon over the ham-stuffed eggs. Add the ketchup and milk as above to the last of the mayonnaise and spoon over the prawn-stuffed eggs. Garnish both dishes with watercress.

Moussaka

☆ ☆   ①   ⊠ ⊠   ⊠ ⊠

Preparation and cooking time:
1 hour 20 minutes, plus 30 minutes for draining
Serving time: *45 minutes-1¼ hours*
SERVES 12

8 large aubergines [eggplants]
salt
5 fl. oz. cooking oil
3 lb. shoulder of lamb, coarsely minced [ground]
3 lb. onions, chopped
2 cloves of garlic, crushed
5 oz. [1¼ cups] flour
2 lb. canned tomatoes
½ teaspoon mixed dried herbs
4 tablespoons chopped parsley
pepper
3 oz. [6 tablespoons] butter
1½ pints [3¾ cups] milk
¾ lb. strong Cheddar cheese, grated

Slice the unpeeled aubergines in ½-inch rounds. Sprinkle with salt and leave for 30 minutes, then drain off the liquid. Fry the aubergines, a few at a time, in some of the oil.
Heat 2 tablespoons of oil in a pan and fry the meat for about 5 minutes, add the onions and garlic and cook for a further 10 minutes. Blend in 2 ounces [½ cup] of the flour, the juice from the can of tomatoes, the herbs and seasoning. Bring to the boil, stirring, and cook for 2 minutes.
Lightly grease one large or two smaller ovenproof dishes. Arrange the aubergine slices, meat mixture and tomato in layers, finishing with a circular pattern of aubergine slices. Melt the butter in a pan, add the remaining flour and cook for a minute, stirring. Gradually blend in the milk and bring to the boil, stirring all the time. Remove from the heat and add the cheese and seasoning. Pour this sauce over the casseroled layers.

Refrigerate, covered, for up to 1-2 days, or deep-freeze.

Heat oven to 375°F (Gas Mark 5, 190°C).
Bake the moussaka before serving. Two small dishes will take 45 minutes or a large dish 1¼ hours.

Savarin

☆ ☆ ☆ ① ①   ⊠ ⊠   ⊠

Preparation and cooking time:
1 hour 25 minutes
Serving time: *minimal*
SERVES 12

½ oz. [1 tablespoon] lard
5 fl. oz. milk plus 5 tablespoons
1 teaspoon sugar
2½ teaspoons dried yeast
12 oz. [3 cups] plain [all-purpose] flour
pinch salt
3 eggs, beaten
4½ oz. [½ cup] butter or margarine, melted
1¼ lb. [2½ cups] sugar
1 pint [2½ cups] water
8 tablespoons rum
2 lb. fresh prepared fruit in season

Grease a 9-inch ring tin well, with the lard. Heat the milk to blood temperature, then turn into a small bowl. Stir in the sugar and sprinkle over the dried yeast. Put into a warm place and leave for about 10 minutes or until the mixture is frothy. Sift the flour and salt into a large mixing bowl. Make a hollow in the flour, pour in the yeast mixture and the beaten eggs and mix with a wooden spoon to a smooth dough. Then beat in the melted and cooled butter, using your hand. Continue to beat the dough for a few minutes by hand until it is really smooth. Turn the dough into the greased tin, cover with a greased polythene [plastic] bag and leave in a warm place for 30-40 minutes, or until the dough has risen almost to the top of the tin.
Heat oven to 425°F (Gas Mark 7, 220°C). Remove the bag and bake the savarin for about 25 minutes or until golden brown and firm. Leave to cool in the tin for 5 minutes, then turn out on to a rack with a plate underneath.
While the savarin is cooking, put the sugar into a saucepan with the water and place over a gentle heat until the sugar has dissolved. Bring to the boil, then remove from the heat and stir in the rum.
Using a fine skewer, make holes all over the savarin and pour over the rum syrup. When all the syrup has been used, pour any which has drained on to the plate back into the pan. Pour over the savarin again. Repeat this until you have only about 5 fl. oz. of syrup left. Place the savarin on a serving dish. Mix the reserved syrup with the prepared fruit, and spoon this into the centre and around the outside of the savarin.

Cover loosely with foil and refrigerate for up to 24 hours. The cooked savarin can be deep-frozen; soak it with the warm syrup after defrosting.

Serve the savarin with plenty of cream.

BARBECUE LUNCH

Marinated Lamb Chops with Barbecue Sauce

This delightful style of entertaining can be lots of fun for everyone – including the cook! The sauce can be made 24 hours ahead, and the chops should be marinated for 24 hours to obtain the full benefit of flavour and tenderizing processes. Prepare the Rillettes and Curd Tarts in advance as well. Then you will be completely prepared and free to turn your attention to your guests, and to the barbecue itself.

If your barbecue equipment is new, try it out on your family first – practice with timing and heat control will ensure success. Almost any barbecue, if you use charcoal as a heating agent, will take at least two hours to gain a sufficient temperature for cooking: wait until the charcoal has turned into a grey ash.

A green or other seasonal salad would make a good accompaniment to the main course, but try to keep the meal simple, to allow a pleasant informality. Iced drinks would be best on a hot summer's day: a lager, and for the children, soft drinks.

Remove the skin and all the bones from the pork and cut into ½-inch cubes. Put them into an ovenproof dish with the thyme, whole garlic and seasoning. Cover and cook for 3 hours.

Place a sieve over a bowl and turn the pork mixture into the sieve. Discard any large pieces of pork fat, then roughly mash the meat, a little at a time, on a board with two forks. Pack the pork firmly into a terrine, then pour the strained juice and most of the fat over the top.

Refrigerate, covered, for up to 1 week, or deep-freeze.

Serve the rillettes with garlic bread.

Garlic Bread: Cream 4 oz. [½ cup] butter with a large crushed clove of garlic and salt and pepper. Take 1 large, or two smaller, French loaves and make diagonal cuts about 2-inches apart, almost down to the base. Spread the garlic butter between these cuts. Wrap the loaves in foil (they can be stored for up to 12 hours) and then heat gently at the edge of a barbecue fire, or in a cool oven.

Marinated Lamb Chops with Barbecue Sauce

☆　　　①①①🗙🗙🗙🗙

Preparation and cooking time:
30 minutes, plus 6 hours to marinate
Serving time: *about 20 minutes*
SERVES 8

6 tablespoons cooking oil
2 teaspoons French mustard
juice of 1 lemon
2 tablespoons soy sauce
2 cloves of garlic, crushed
salt and pepper
8 large lamb chops
Barbecue Sauce:
2 tablespoons oil
8 tablespoons peanut butter
½ pint [1¼ cups] tomato ketchup
6 tablespoons Worcestershire sauce
1 clove garlic, crushed
salt and pepper

Mix together the oil, mustard, lemon juice, soy sauce, garlic and seasoning. Put into a large, shallow dish and add the chops.
Heat the oil for the sauce in a pan. Add the peanut butter and continue heating

gently, stirring occasionally, until the peanut butter begins to thicken and darkens slightly. Immediately remove from the heat and stir in the remaining ingredients.

Leave the chops to marinate for at least 6 hours in a cool place, or preferably for 24 hours. Do not deep-freeze. The sauce should be made at least 2 hours before it is required and can be stored in a cool place for up to 24 hours, or deep-frozen.

Grill the chops over a barbecue fire for about 20 minutes, turning once or twice. Reheat the sauce gently in a pan at the edge of the fire.

Spiced Curd Tarts

☆ ☆　　①① 🗙　　🗙

Preparation and cooking time:
50 minutes
Serving time: about *10 minutes*
MAKES 16 tarts

8 oz. short crust pastry (see page 61)
2 oz. [½ cup] stoned or seedless raisins
2 oz. [4 tablespoons] butter
2 oz. [4 tablespoons] castor [fine] sugar
grated zest of ½ a lemon
1 egg, lightly beaten
1 tablespoon self-raising flour sifted with ½ teaspoon ground cinnamon
½ lb. [1 cup] curd or cream cheese
2 tablespoons milk

Heat oven to 350°F (Gas Mark 4, 180°C).
Make up the pastry (see page 61). Roll it out and cut into circles, about 3-inches in diameter. Use to line 16 patty [muffin] tins.
Lightly prick the pastry and put a few raisins in the bottom of each tart.
Cream the butter, sugar and lemon zest until soft and light. Gradually beat in the egg, then the flour, cheese and milk. Divide the mixture between the pastry cases and bake for about 30 minutes or until the filling is well-risen and set.

Allow the pastries to cool, then refrigerate, covered, for up to 3 days, or deep-freeze.

The tarts are best served warm. Replace them in the patty tins, and either reheat gently at the edge of the barbecue fire or in a cool oven.

Rillettes

☆ ☆　　①　　🗙🗙🗙🗙

Preparation and cooking time: *4 hours*
Serving time: *minimal*
SERVES 8

4 lb. lean belly of pork
sprig of fresh thyme (or ¼ teaspoon dried thyme)
1-2 cloves of garlic
salt and pepper

Heat oven to 300°F (Gas Mark 1-2, 150°C).

MEAL FOR AN EVENING OUT

A late-night meal needs to be both light and easily digestible – and, of course, also needs to be able to be served in as short a time as possible, after the return home.

The first and last course of this menu are planned to be ready-to-serve, and the main course of Pork Hongroise can be gently re-heating while the first course is being eaten. Coming home late after any sort of outing is a good reason for serving a quick meal such as this; and if you have a busy week ahead of you at any time, it would be helpful to prepare in advance for this sort of eventuality. The dishes are elegant ones and very suitable for guests, but are not too rich or expensive in their ingredients to make a sensible family meal too.

Zeilook

☆ ☆   ① ①   ⊠ ⊠   ⧗

Preparation and cooking time:
1 hour 5 minutes
Serving time: *minimal*
SERVES 4

5 fl. oz. olive oil
1 onion, chopped
2 aubergines [eggplants], **sliced**
2 courgettes [zucchini], **sliced**
2 large tomatoes, peeled and sliced
2 teaspoons chopped parsley
good pinch of cayenne pepper
salt
To garnish:
green olives

Heat the oil in a pan and fry the onion

---

opposite: centre: Pineapple Salad with Kirsch
left: Pork Hongroise
served in dishes: Zeilook

for 5 minutes. Add the aubergines and courgettes, cover, and cook gently for 10 minutes. Then add the remaining ingredients, and simmer for about 20 minutes in a covered pan. Mash the mixture with a vegetable masher to break it down, and cook at a high temperature in an open pan for about 5 minutes, stirring frequently until the mixture thickens. Remove from the heat, mash again, and cook the mixture for a further 5 minutes, stirring all the time. Remove from the heat, taste, and adjust the seasoning. Turn into a dish and garnish with olives.

Refrigerate, covered, for at least 3 hours, or up to 4 days. It will deep-freeze.

Serve the Zeilook chilled with hot toast.

Pork Hongroise with Sour Cream

☆   ① ①   ⊠   ⧗

Preparation and cooking time:
50 minutes
Serving time: *about 20 minutes*
SERVES 4

1½ lb. pork fillet
2 tablespoons oil
1 oz. [2 tablespoons] **butter**
1 onion, chopped
1 tablespoon paprika
1 oz. [4 tablespoons] **flour**
½ pint [1¼ cups] **water**
4 tablespoons sherry
1 stock cube
¼ lb. mushrooms
salt and pepper
5 fl. oz. sour cream, or double
  [heavy] **cream mixed with 1**
  tablespoon lemon juice

Cut the pork into 1½-inch pieces. Heat the oil and butter in a pan and fry the

meat on all sides for about 5 minutes. Remove the meat from the pan with a draining spoon and put on one side. *Add* the onion to the pan and fry for 5 minutes. Stir in the paprika and flour and cook for a further 2 minutes. Gradually stir in the water. Bring to the boil, stirring all the time, then add the sherry, meat, stock cube and mushrooms. Cover and simmer for 20 minutes or until the meat is tender. Taste and adjust the seasoning.

Refrigerate, covered, for up to 1-2 days, or deep-freeze.

Reheat the pork gently and just before serving, stir in the sour cream.

Pineapple Salad with Kirsch

☆   ① ① ①   ⊠   ⧗

Preparation time: *about 20 minutes*
Serving time: *minimal*
SERVES 4

2 small pineapples
¼ lb. black grapes
1 banana
1 pear
2-3 tablespoons kirsch
castor [fine] **sugar**

Cut the pineapples in half. Scoop out the flesh using first a knife and then a spoon; take care to keep the pineapple cases intact. Chop the pineapple flesh and discard the core. Put it into a bowl together with any pineapple juice. Halve the grapes and remove the pips. Peel and slice the banana; peel, core and slice the pear. Mix all the fruit together in a bowl, then add the kirsch. Sweeten to taste with sugar. Pile the fruit back into the pineapple cases.

Refrigerate for up to 8 hours. Do not deep-freeze.

Serve chilled with fresh cream.

Note: The kirsch may be omitted (in which case the banana and pear should be dipped in lemon juice to preserve the colour), or brandy or white wine could be used instead.
If small pineapples are not available, use 1 medium-sized one. Cut off the top, scoop out the flesh, then pile the fruit salad back inside the pineapple shell and replace the lid, or put into 4 small dishes for serving.

AUTO-TIMER MEAL

The main course of this menu would make a satisfying and complete meal in itself, if need be. And its great advantage is that it is all cooked in a single ovenproof dish, ready to serve. For a more elaborate meal the Borstch and the Chocolate Soufflé are ideal accompaniments, and both may be prepared in advance, needing only a few minutes' attention before their serving times. If a wine is needed, a Médoc would blend very well with all three courses.

Soufflé are ideal accompaniments, Médoc would blend very well with Auto-timer controls can be an immensely useful piece of cookery equipment, and if your oven has such a device use it as often as you can. A casserole such as this pot roast is an ideal choice because it needs no extra care during the baking period – and jacket potatoes may easily be added to the oven before the controls are set. But do remember that some foods are less suitable for auto-timing – any which will discolour, or in which the texture flavour or quality may suffer, should not be used. For further suggestions on auto-timer cookery see the notes on page 8.

Borstch

☆ ① ▨ ◪

Preparation and cooking time:
55 minutes
Serving time: *about 10 minutes*
SERVES 4

1 lb. raw beetroot [beets]
2 pints [5 cups] stock or water
1 teaspoon sugar
juice of ½ a lemon
salt
2 hard-boiled eggs
½ **cucumber**
2 spring onions [scallions], **chopped**
5 fl. oz. sour cream, or double [heavy] **cream mixed with 1 tablespoon lemon juice**

Peel the beetroot and dice into ½-inch pieces. Put these into a saucepan with the water, bring to the boil and simmer for 30 minutes.
Strain the mixture and add the sugar, lemon juice and salt.

Refrigerate for up to 4 days, or deep-freeze.

Shell and quarter the eggs. Peel and slice the cucumber. Add the onions, eggs, and cucumber to the soup just before serving. Top each bowl of soup with a large spoonful of sour cream.

Note: If the Borstch is not a very good colour after cooking for 30 minutes, add a little more raw beetroot and cook for a further 2-3 minutes, then strain.

Pot-roasted Stuffed Chicken

☆ ① ▨ ◪ ◪

Preparation and cooking time:
30 minutes
Serving time: *about 2 hours*
SERVES 6

4 oz. [1 cup] rice
salt
1 oz. [¼ cup] sultanas or raisins
2 sticks celery, finely chopped
1 oz. [2 tablespoons] butter
4-5 lb. roasting chicken
1 lb. button onions
1 lb. small tomatoes
1 lb. carrots
4 tablespoons water
pepper

Cook the rice in boiling salted water until just tender. Drain. Stir in the sultanas, celery and butter and use this mixture to stuff the chicken. Peel the onions and tomatoes. Peel or scrape the carrots; if they are young leave them whole; if they are large old ones, cut into quarters lengthwise. Put the vegetables with the water in the bottom of a large casserole and season with salt and pepper. Place the stuffed chicken on the top.

Either store at room temperature for up to 6 hours (or in the oven if using an auto-timer), or refrigerate for up to 24 hours. Do not deep-freeze.

Heat oven to 350°F (Gas Mark 4, 180°C).

Cook the chicken for 2 hours. Serve with small baked potatoes in their jackets, which can be cooked at the same time as the chicken.

Chocolate Soufflé

☆ ☆ ① ① ▨ ◪

Preparation time: *40 minutes*
Serving time: *10 minutes*
SERVES 4-6

¼ **lb. plain** [semi-sweet] **chocolate**
2 tablespoons milk
3 eggs, separated
3 oz. [6 tablespoons] castor [fine] **sugar**
2 teaspoons powdered gelatine
2 tablespoons water
½ **pint [1¼ cups] double** [heavy] **cream, lightly whipped**
To decorate:
chopped nuts
Maraschino cherries

First prepare the soufflé dish; a 6-inch dish would be the most suitable. Cut a band of greaseproof [waxed] paper three times the depth of the dish. Fold this in half to give a double thickness and brush the part which will stand above the dish with melted butter. Tie or pin the band of paper very securely around the outside of the soufflé dish. *Break* the chocolate into pieces and put into a bowl with the milk, egg yolks and sugar. Stand the bowl over a pan of gently simmering water and stir until the chocolate has melted, then whisk until thick and creamy. Soften the gelatine in the cold water, then stand over a pan of hot water, until dissolved. Add to the chocolate mixture. Put on one side and allow to thicken slightly. Stiffly whisk the egg whites and fold first the cream, and then the egg whites into the chocolate mixture. Turn into the prepared soufflé dish.

Refrigerate until set, and store for up to 2 days, or deep-freeze.

Carefully remove the paper from the soufflé. Press the chopped nuts against the side of the soufflé, using a palette knife, and decorate the top with the cherries.

---

opposite: top: Pot-roasted Stuffed Chicken
left: Borstch

WEEKEND GUESTS

Having friends to stay should be an enjoyable time for everyone – and not an occasion to be dreaded because of the extra work involved, especially at meal-times. The next six pages are full of suggestions for recipes to prepare ahead of time, so that you may greet your guests with confidence – and wave goodbye on Sunday evening hoping they'll come again soon!

below: Sausage Jambalaya, Apple Snow

FRIDAY

Onions Monégasque

☆ ① ⊠ ▮

Preparation and cooking time:
50 minutes
Serving time: *minimal*
SERVES 4

5 fl. oz. water
juice of ½ a lemon
2 tablespoons oil
sprig of fresh thyme
1 clove of garlic, crushed
2 level tablespoons tomato purée
salt and pepper
1 lb. button onions
2 oz. [½ cup] raisins

Put the water, lemon juice, oil, thyme, garlic, tomato purée and seasoning into a saucepan, and bring to the boil. Peel the onions, and add to the pan with the raisins. Simmer for 30 minutes.

Refrigerate, covered, for up to 2-3 days, or deep-freeze.

Serve chilled with Melba Toast.

Stuffed Cannelloni with Cheese Sauce

☆ ① ⊠ ▮

Preparation and cooking time:
30 minutes
Serving time: *about 30 minutes*
SERVES 4

8 cannelloni tubes
salt
1 tablespoon oil
3½ oz. [7 tablespoons] butter
1 onion, chopped
4 oz. [½ cup] mushrooms, chopped
½ green pepper, chopped
4 oz. [½ cup] ham, chopped
1 egg
1 oz. [¼ cup] grated Parmesan cheese
pepper

1½ oz. [⅓ cup] flour
¾ pint [2 cups] milk
4 oz. [1 cup] Gruyere or Cheddar cheese, grated

Cook the cannelloni in a large pan of boiling salted water until just tender. Drain.
Heat the oil and 1 ounce [2 tablespoons] of the butter in a pan and gently cook the onion, mushrooms and pepper. Remove from the heat and stir in the ham, egg and Parmesan cheese. Use this mixture to stuff the cannelloni—a teaspoon works best. Using the remaining butter, flour and milk, make up a white sauce (see page 63). Remove from the heat and stir in the Gruyére or Cheddar cheese. Season to taste.
Spoon about half the sauce into an ovenproof dish, then arrange the cannelloni on top. Pour over the remaining sauce.

Refrigerate, covered, for up to 24 hours, or deep-freeze.

Heat oven to 375 °F (Gas Mark 5, 190 °C).
Uncover and cook the cannelloni for 30 minutes, until the sauce is golden brown and the pasta is piping hot.

Oranges in Caramel Sauce

☆ ☆ ① ⊠ ⊠ ⊠ ▮

Preparation and cooking time:
50 minutes
Serving time: *minimal*
SERVES 4

3 oz. [6 tablespoons] butter or margarine

6 oranges
½ pint [1¼ cups] water
8 oz. [1 cup] sugar

Pare the zest carefully from one of the oranges, and cut this into thin strips. Soak in 5 fl. oz. of the water for 1 hour, then simmer gently for 20 minutes.
Cut away the peel and white pith from all the oranges, and cut the flesh into ¼-inch slices. Place these in a serving dish. Put the sugar and the remainder of the water into a saucepan. Heat gently, stirring until the sugar has dissolved, then boil rapidly until the mixture turns golden brown. Remove from the heat, then add the strained liquid from the orange zest. Replace over the heat and stir until blended, then add the orange zest. Pour the caramel sauce over the oranges.

Refrigerate for at least 8 hours, or up to 4 days. The oranges can be deep-frozen.

Serve with finger biscuits [cookies].

Prepare For Breakfast The Night Before
This will help enormously when you have guests to stay. Set the table, adding cereals and so forth, and prepare any grapefruit if that is being served. Put bacon ready on the grill [broiler], and have frying pans and utensils out. Scrambled eggs would be a good choice: lightly beat the eggs, add the milk, salt and pepper, and leave covered in a bowl. The Sunday breakfast Kedgeree could be made beforehand and reheated – an excellent idea if you have an auto-timer to set ahead.
And put the toaster on a side table, so that everyone can make their own.

SATURDAY

Saturday lunch
Sausage Jambalaya

☆ ① ⊠ ▮

Preparation and cooking time:
55 minutes
Serving time: *about 30 minutes*
SERVES 6

2 large onions, chopped
12 oz. [2 cups] long-grain rice
1½ pints [3¾ cups] water
1½ lb. pork sausages
1 stock cube
salt
½ lb. frozen mixed vegetables
¼ lb. mushrooms, sliced
4 oz. [1 cup] grated cheese

Melt 2 ounces [4 tablespoons] of the butter or margarine in a pan, add the onions, cover and cook gently for 10 minutes. Stir in the rice and fry gently for 2-3 minutes. Add the water and bring to the boil. Halve the sausages and add these to the pan with the stock cube and seasoning. Cover and cook for about 10 minutes. Stir in the mixed vegetables and mushrooms, and cook for a further 15 minutes or until all the liquid has been absorbed. Remove the pan from the heat and stir in the remaining butter.

Refrigerate, covered, for up to 1-2 days, or deep-freeze.

Heat oven to 350°F (Gas Mark 4, 180°C).
Turn the Jambalaya into an ovenproof serving dish. Cover with foil and cook for 30 minutes or until piping hot. Serve sprinkled with the grated cheese.

Apple Snow

Preparation and cooking time:
45 minutes
Serving time: *minimal*
SERVES 6

5 fl. oz. water
4 oz. [½ cup] sugar
peeled zest of 1 lemon
2 lb. cooking apples
2 teaspoons powdered gelatine
3 eggs, separated

Put the water, sugar and lemon zest into a saucepan and heat gently until the sugar has dissolved. Peel, core and slice the apples, add to the pan, cover and cook gently until the apples are

reduced to a purée. Remove from the heat.
While the apples are cooking, soften the gelatine in 2 tablespoons of cold water, then add to the hot apple purée. Stir until it has dissolved, then beat in the egg yolks, one at a time. Stiffly whisk the egg whites and fold into the apple mixture when it is cool, but not set. Turn into a serving dish.

Refrigerate, covered, for up to 2 days. It can be deep frozen, but may lose some of its light texture.

Serve the apple snow with crisp biscuits [cookies].

Saturday dinner
Artichoke soup
Stuffed baked sea bass
Blackcurrant sorbet

SUNDAY

Sunday breakfast
Kedgeree

Preparation and cooking time:
40 minutes
Serving time: *about 30 minutes*
SERVES 4-6

¾ lb. smoked haddock
1¼ pints [3 cups] water
a few parsley stalks
a small bayleaf
1 lemon
a few peppercorns
2 oz. [4 tablespoons] butter
1 small onion, chopped
8 oz. [1¼ cups] long-grain rice
2 eggs, hard-boiled
salt and pepper

Put the haddock into a saucepan with the water, parsley stalks, bayleaf, half the lemon cut into slices, and the peppercorns. Poach for about 8 minutes, until the fish flakes easily with a fork. Remove the fish, and skin and flake it. Then strain the fish stock, measure, and make it up to 1 pint [2½

cups] with more water if necessary. *Melt* half the butter in a pan, and fry the onion and rice gently, for about 5 minutes. Add the fish stock, cover, and simmer gently for about 20 minutes until the rice is tender and the liquid has been absorbed. Chop the hard-boiled eggs and stir this into the rice, together with the juice from the remaining lemon half and the rest of the butter. Season to taste.

Turn the mixture into an ovenproof dish, cover, and refrigerate for up to 2 days.

Heat oven to 350°F (Gas Mark 4, 180°C).
Cook for 30 minutes, until piping hot.

Sunday lunch
Try this topping recipe with a roast leg of lamb, cooked in your usual way, and served with roast potatoes and a green vegetable, such as broccoli or cauliflower. Follow with the Lemon Meringue Pie.

Garlic and Herb Topping

3 oz. [6 tablespoons] butter
2 oz. [½ cup] fresh white breadcrumbs
1 clove of garlic, crushed
1 tablespoon chopped parsley
½ teaspoon fresh rosemary, finely chopped (or a pinch of dried rosemary)

Cream the butter, and then add the rest of the ingredients. Blend together well.

Refrigerate in a covered container for up to 1 week, or deep-freeze.

Half-way through the roasting time, spread the topping over the joint, and complete the roasting (do not cover the joint after the topping is added). If children are to be served who may not like the topping, spread it over only half of the joint.

BASIC RECIPES & METHODS

for dishes to prepare the day before

Shortcrust Pastry

Preparation time: *20 minutes*
MAKES 8 oz. pastry

8 oz. [2 cups] **plain** [all-purpose] **flour**
pinch of salt
4 oz. [½ cup] **fat, this can be butter,**
margarine, or a mixture of
margarine and lard
2-4 tablespoons cold water

Sift the flour and salt into a bowl. Cut
the fat into small pieces and using your
fingertips, rub it into the flour until the
mixture resembles fine breadcrumbs.
Add the water, using a palette knife to
cut and stir the mixture thoroughly, so
that it clings together leaving the sides
of the bowl clean. Put the pastry on to a
floured board or working surface, and
knead very lightly so that you have a
smooth, round ball. Roll out, and use
as required.
It is very important when making short
crust pastry to ensure that you do not
overhandle the mixture, and that you
do not add too much water, as this will
make the pastry tough, and cause it to
shrink considerably during the cooking.

For 4 ounces of pastry
Use 4 ounces [1 cup] of plain flour, a
pinch of salt, 2 ounces [4 tablespoons] of
fat, and up to 2 tablespoons of cold water.

Flan Pastry

For 8 ounces of pastry
Use the shortcrust pastry recipe, but
substitute 2 egg yolks for some of the
water.

For 4 ounces of pastry
Use the quantities for 4 ounces of
shortcrust pastry, but use an egg yolk
mixed with about 1 tablespoon of cold
water.

For 6 ounces of pastry

Use 6 ounces [1½ cups] of flour, a pinch
of salt, 3 ounces [6 tablespoons] of fat,
and an egg yolk mixed with 1-2
tablespoons of cold water.

To make a flan case

Place the flan ring on an upturned
baking tray, or use a sandwich tin. For
a deep 6-inch or a shallow 7-inch flan
you need 4 ounces of pastry, for a deep
7-inch to a shallow 9-inch flan you need
6 ounces of pastry and for a deep 9-inch
to a deep 12-inch flan, you need 8
ounces of pastry.
Roll the pastry out evenly into as neat
a circle as possible, about 2-inches
larger than the diameter of the flan
ring. Using the rolling pin for support,
carefully lift the pastry into the flan
ring. Then, with your index finger,
press the pastry down into the flan ring
and, if using a fluted flan ring, into the
flutes. To neaten the edge of the flan,
place the rolling pin across the centre of
the flan ring, and roll away from
yourself in one short stroke across the
top, so that excess pastry is cut off by
the pressure. Turn the flan around, and
repeat the process. Now either fill the
flan and bake, or bake blind.

To bake a flan case blind

Preparation and cooking time:
about 35 minutes

Heat oven to 400°F (Gas Mark 6,
200°C).
Put a sheet of greaseproof [waxed]
paper or foil, about 4-inches larger than
the diameter of the flan, into the bottom
of the flan case, fitting it gently to the
shape. Fill with raw rice, dried
breadcrusts or baking beans.
Put into the oven, and bake for 10-15
minutes, or until the pastry is set firm.
Remove the paper and beans, and bake
for a further 5-10 minutes to dry out
the base. The beans should be allowed

to cool, then put into a suitable
container. They can then be used again.

Note: If you are using a china flan dish
you will probably find that the flan case
takes slightly longer to cook and that
fillings also take longer to set. This is
because china does not transmit the
heat as fast as metal.

Suet Crust Pastry

Preparation time: *10 minutes*
MAKES 8 oz. pastry

8 oz. [2 cups] **self-raising flour (or**
plain [all-purpose] **flour with 2**
teaspoons baking powder)
½ teaspoon salt
4 oz. [½ cup] **shredded beef suet**
about 5 fl. oz. water

Sift together the flour, the baking
powder, if used, and the salt. Add the
suet and mix with water until the
mixture binds together and leaves the
sides of the bowl clean.
Use in recipes as directed.

Lining a Bowl with Suet Crust
Pastry

Roll the pastry out to form a round
large enough to fill the bowl. Cut out a
quarter of the round, and put this to
one side for the lid. Lower the
remaining pastry into the greased bowl,
and seal the joins together. Trim the
top of the pastry and add these pieces
to the quarter reserved for the top.

To cover a bowl for steaming

Take two pieces of greased greaseproof
[waxed] paper (or one piece of greased
foil), each at least 6-inches wider than
the diameter of the top of the basin.
Make a pleat in the centre, about 1-inch
wide, to allow for the pudding to

for dishes to prepare the day before

expand. If greaseproof paper is used, put it over the top of the pudding bowl, pull taut, and tie it in place with string. If foil is used, it may either be tied into place like the paper, or its edges turned firmly under to form a taut covering.

Hot Water Crust Pastry

Preparation time: *20 minutes*
MAKES 12 oz. pastry

12 oz. [3 cups] plain [all-purpose] **flour**
1 teaspoon salt
4½ oz. [½ cup] lard
7½ fl. oz. [nearly 1 cup] water

Sift the flour and salt together into a mixing bowl, and put in a warm place. Put the lard and water into a saucepan and place over a moderate heat. Bring this gradually to the boil, and as soon as it is boiling rapidly, pour immediately into the centre of the warmed flour. Beat well with a wooden spoon until the mixture clings together in a ball, leaving the sides of the basin clean. Turn out on to a lightly floured working surface and knead well to a smooth dough.
It is important to use this dough while it is still hot and pliable. If it is left to get too cold before handling it will crack badly and become difficult to work. Keep the pastry warm and soft by placing under the hot, upturned mixing bowl.

To Prepare a Cake Tin

For a light sponge cake, the cake tins may either be lightly greased and floured, or the whole tin greased and the bottom lined with a circle or square of greased greaseproof [waxed] paper. For richer fruit cakes, the bottom and sides of the cake tin should be lined with one or two layers of greased greaseproof paper.

Victoria Sandwich Mixture

Preparation and cooking time:
45 minutes
MAKES 2 x 6-in. sandwich cakes

4 oz. [1 cup] self-raising flour or
 plain [all-purpose] flour, sifted
 with 1 teaspoon baking powder
4 oz. [½ cup] butter or margarine
4 oz. [½ cup] castor [fine] sugar
2 eggs, lightly beaten
¼ teaspoon vanilla essence

Sift the flour. Cream the butter and sugar together until white, light and fluffy. Very gradually beat in the lightly beaten eggs and vanilla essence, adding a tablespoon of the sieved flour with the last amount of egg. Carefully fold in the flour.
Turn the mixture into two 6-inch prepared sandwich tins (see below) and bake in a fairly hot oven for 20-25 minutes or until the cakes spring back when lightly pressed with the tip of the finger.
Allow to cool in the tin for 5 minutes, then remove to a wire rack for final cooling. Sandwich together with jam, butter icing or cream.

For a 3 egg mixture
Use 6 ounces [1½ cups] of flour, 6 ounces [¾ cup] of fat, and 6 ounces [¾ cup] of sugar with 3 eggs, and ¼ teaspoon of vanilla essence.

Quick Rough Puff Pastry

Preparation time:
15 minutes, plus 20 minutes to chill
MAKES 8 oz. pastry

8 oz. [2 cups] plain [all-purpose] **flour**
pinch of salt
3 oz. [6 tablespoons] lard
3 oz. [6 tablespoons] margarine
up to 5 fl. oz. water

Sift the flour and salt into a bowl. Cut the fat up roughly into small pieces, about ½-inch cubes using two round-bladed knifes in a scissor action. Add these to the flour, and mix to a soft dough with the water. Roll out on a floured board to an oblong about 5-inches by 12-inches. Bring the top third of the pastry down and the bottom third of the pastry up, to make an envelope shape. Turn the pastry at right angles and repeat the rolling and folding three more times. Chill for about 20 minutes, and then use as directed.

For 4 ounces of pastry
Use 4 ounces [1 cup] of flour, a pinch of salt, 1½ ounces [3 tablespoons] of lard, 1½ ounces [3 tablespoons] of margarine, and up to 3 fluid ounces of water.

Pancake Batter

Preparation time: *about 30 minutes*
MAKES 8 x 7-in. pancakes

4 oz. [1 cup] flour
¼ teaspoon salt
1 egg
10 fl. oz. [1¼ cups] milk

Sift the flour and salt into a bowl. Add the egg, then gradually beat in half the milk to make a smooth batter. Beat in the remaining milk, then pour the batter into a jug.

For a rich Pancake Batter:
Using 4 ounces [1 cup] of flour, add 2 eggs, a generous 5 fl. oz. of milk and 1 ounce [2 tablespoons] of melted butter.

To Make Pancakes

Lightly grease a frying pan with oil, lard or butter and put over the heat until hot. Quickly pour in enough batter, (about 3 tablespoons) to cover the bottom of the pan thinly, tilting the pan to achieve an even coverage. Cook until the underside of the pancake is golden brown, turn, and cook on the other side.

Using Gelatine

First soften the gelatine in cold water or other liquid.
Allow about 4 tablespoons of liquid to $\frac{1}{2}$ ounce [2 tablespoons] of powdered gelatine. Pour the liquid into a small bowl and sprinkle over the gelatine. Leave to soften for about 5 minutes, then dissolve the gelatine either by standing the bowl over a pan of hot water, or by adding it to a very hot liquid or purée.

To Make Stock

Stock can be made from raw or cooked bones. It is particularly wasteful to throw away the bones of a chicken, turkey or duck, as these can very easily be used to make a nourishing soup. Put the bones (beef marrow bones make particularly good stock) into a large saucepan and cover them with cold salted water. Bring to the boil and skim. Cover, and cook very slowly for about 3 hours, topping up with a little extra water if necessary. Strain the stock from the bones, and skim again. Keep the stock in the refrigerator until required, but boil up again every 2-3 days, to keep it wholesome. It may also be deep-frozen. Vegetables may be added to the stock to give extra flavour, but in this case the stock will not keep as well. The best and most usual additions are carrot, onion, turnip, celery and mushroom stalks—and a bouquet garni of herbs may also be added.

White Sauce

Preparation and cooking time: *16 minutes*
MAKES $\frac{1}{2}$ pint [1$\frac{1}{4}$ cups], coating consistency

1 oz. [2 tablespoons] **butter or**
    margarine
1 oz. [4 tablespoons] **flour**
$\frac{1}{2}$ **pint [1$\frac{1}{4}$ cups] milk, or milk and fish**
    or meat stock to make that amount
salt and pepper

Melt the butter or margarine in a saucepan. Stir in the flour and cook for about a minute over a low heat—this mixture is known as a 'roux'. Remove it from the heat and gradually stir in the milk, or the milk and fish or meat stock mixture.
Return to the heat and bring to the boil, stirring all the time. Cook for about 3 minutes and season to taste.

Note: For a thin, pouring white sauce, use only $\frac{1}{2}$ an ounce [1 tablespoon] of fat and flour [2 tablespoons] to 10 fl. oz. [1$\frac{1}{4}$ cups] milk. For a thick panada, used as a basis for soufflés and fish cakes, use 2 ounces of fat [$\frac{1}{4}$ cup] and flour [$\frac{1}{2}$ cup] to 10 fl. oz. [1$\frac{1}{4}$ cups] milk.

French Dressing

Preparation time: *5 minutes*

The ingredients of French Dressing and the proportion of vinegar to oil is very largely a matter of personal taste, but this is a good basic recipe which will give enough dressing to toss a salad for 4 people.

$\frac{1}{4}$ **teaspoon French mustard**
pinch sugar
pinch salt
freshly milled black pepper
1 tablespoon vinegar
2 tablespoons oil

Either mix together the mustard, sugar, salt, pepper and vinegar in a basin, and then add in the oil, or put all the ingredients into a screw-topped jar and shake well. In either case, make sure all ingredients are thoroughly combined.

Mayonnaise

Preparation time: *10 minutes*
MAKES $\frac{1}{2}$ pint [1$\frac{1}{4}$ cups]

2 egg yolks
$\frac{1}{2}$ **teaspoon dry mustard**
$\frac{1}{2}$ **teaspoon salt**
pepper
2 tablespoons wine vinegar or lemon
    juice
$\frac{1}{2}$ **pint [1$\frac{1}{4}$ cups] oil**

For the best results, have all the ingredients at room temperature. You can make mayonnaise from eggs straight from the refrigerator, but there will be a much greater chance of it curdling.
Beat the egg yolks with the mustard, salt, pepper and 1 tablespoon vinegar. Use either a balloon whisk or a wooden spoon for this, whichever you find easier. Now gradually beat in the oil, literally drop by drop, until you have added about half of it and the mixture looks thick and shiny.
At this stage the oil can be added a little more quickly. Add the remaining vinegar when all the oil has been incorporated. If by chance you have added the oil too quickly at the beginning and the mixture does curdle, beat a fresh egg yolk in another bowl, and beat the curdled mixture into this, a teaspoonful at a time.

DISHES TO COOK IN THIRTY MINUTES

The number of meals a housewife must serve every year amounts to a very impressive total. And if you also consider the number of hours which must be spent in that year on planning dishes and menus, on shopping for the ingredients and on preparing the food for cooking, then it becomes all too obvious just how much of our working time is spent on the food which we and our families eat.

And yet, how much more fortunate we are today than were our ancestors when it comes to food preparation. Certainly today, with the help of modern kitchen equipment as well as a host of methods for keeping foods in a near-to-natural state, a cook's choice is much easier and certainly more enjoyable than it was in the past. Even as comparatively recently as the beginning of the eighteenth century only one main method of preserving fresh food for later consumption was used—that of salting and curing. Occasionally, some foods were dried, and for the wealthy there was also the possibility of adding a large proportion of sugary or spicy mixtures to foods to prevent decay. But imagine how dreary meals must have been for the greater part of the year.

All our modern methods of food preservation—canning, bottling, freezing and dehydrating—have evolved from later efforts to improve on these earliest preservatives. Indeed, the result is that the range of convenience foods available might almost appear confusing in its variety—but for the cook in a hurry life has never been so good.

Perhaps, in a sense, it is even a little too good. Sometimes, for many of us, the range of ready-to-use foods is a little too closely related to the 'just add water' class. We all like to have our work simplified where possible, but no cook who truly cares about food always wants to serve up

meals in which her talents have played little or no part—for then she will miss out entirely on the satisfaction and creative stimulus which comes from cooking and serving truly interesting and delicious dishes. For those who find that they must often work against time to prepare a meal and that the range of convenience foods available seems to lack a certain variety, we offer many quick, tasty suggestions. Naturally you will sometimes want to serve canned and packaged foods—they are often very good and are almost always quick and simple to prepare. But we think you will also want to add something of your own to these manufactured products— even if it's just some sizzling hot croûtons scattered on a packet soup or a few spoonsfuls of cream to float on the top of each bowl. Or, why not try sprinkling some freshly chopped parsley or chives into a packet sauce or mixing some extra chunks of freshly cooked vegetables with a canned stew? In addition to such suggestions, the recipes presented here make full use of fresh foods which cook quickly: fish, eggs, finely chopped vegetables and meats, and so forth. But for your own convenience and peace of mind, the best cook's aid you can acquire is a well-stocked storecupboard (in fact, what every kitchen should possess however much time the cook has to spend).

This is simply an essential for all those who need to cook a meal every evening and to think about breakfasts and lunches too. It is hardly sensible to shop every day for all the ingredients you will need for the next meal—this is tiresome, time-consuming, and also makes for far too heavy a load. Very special meals may be an exception, but in general it is much more practical to plan to spend one shopping day a week—or every two weeks, or even once a month—

shopping for basic food stuffs to replenish (or perhaps to start off) your stocks. In this way you will quickly learn to adjust your list to suit your own requirements (we suggest you start with the check lists supplied at the end of this section) and you will be far less likely to run out of salt, flour, canned tomatoes—or whatever is your particular 'blindspot'. If you have a basic list it can quickly be checked through against the contents of your cupboard, before that special shopping trip.

Of course, not everyone has an unlimited amount of storage space which may be used—and certainly we don't all have super floor-to-ceiling cupboards to spare. Your own individual limitations must be allowed for.

In the same way it would be foolish to follow our suggested stock list blindly, without first evaluating it on a personal level. (Do you and your family eat much rice? Or do you find pastas a more interesting accompaniment? Do you bake enough to need different flours, sugars and spices? Do you use dried fruit?) It is in just this way that our 'standard' lists provide a check against which your own list may be made—and you will end up always having a sensible amount of food ready for use in the kitchen, to prevent you from running out of frequently used items.

The foods in our basic lists divide into three section headings— dried and packaged food, canned and bottled food, and herbs, spices and flavourings.

Dried and packaged food

Beverages: tea (China, Indian or herbal blends), coffee (instant, ground or whole beans), and any others of your own choice, such as drinking chocolate. It is a good idea to have dried milk

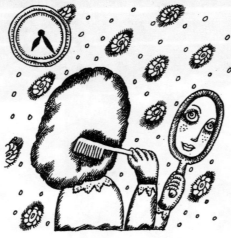

powder on hand, or one of the special additives for coffee or tea, as well.

Flours: the basics—plain [all purpose], self-raising, wholemeal or wheatmeal (sometimes stone-ground), cornflour [cornstarch]. The special ones—such as rice flour, corn meal, matzo meal, potato, soya or barley flour, arrowroot and so forth.

Baking accompaniments: baking powder, gelatine, dried yeast, bicarbonate of soda [baking soda], oatmeal or rolled oats.

Salt: table salt, cooking or rock salt (usually coarser than table salt and without the free-running additives) or sea salt.

Sugar: granulated, castor [fine], icing [confectioners'], as well as the brown sugars, demerara, coffee crystals and cube or lump sugar.

Rice: long-grain or 'Patna-type', brown or 'whole' rice, 'pudding' or 'Carolina-type' rice—and instant or fast-cooking varieties which have been specially processed.

Pasta: spaghetti, macaroni, noodles, tagliatelle, vermicelli, and all the shape variations (shells, hoops and so forth) which are available. There is also 'sheet' pasta for making lasagne and tube pasta for canneloni.

Dried fruit: currants and sultanas, raisins, apricots, dates, prunes, figs—and the more exotic varieties sometimes available such as bananas, peaches, pears and plums. These last are sometimes referred to as 'evaporated' rather than 'dried'.

Vegetables: mushrooms and sliced onions are both widely available, and make good stand-bys. Freeze-dried vegetables (peas, carrots and so forth) are a matter of taste as an alternative to fresh or frozen. Instant potato powder mixes are also widely available and are quite tasty if made with plenty of milk and butter. The wide range of dried beans available today (large butter [dried lima] beans, haricot beans, brown, black and black-eyed beans or peas and so forth) are not an essential part of our list, since all need a time-consuming pre-cooking soak. We have included the canned varieties where appropriate in the next section.

Soups and sauces: packet soups are mainly in the vegetable range, and can be added dry to stews and casseroles as well as made up into liquid. Packet sauces, dips, mixes and so forth are readily available and usually very good value for money—as well as being fast to make.

Meat: salami, mortadella, chorizo and numerous other varieties from many countries and with many different flavours and textures. Find your favourite by taste trials before buying a whole sausage, though.

Canned and bottled food

Vegetables: the ubiquitous tomato (whole, or as purée, paste, sauce, ketchup or juice), and a very wide range of other prepared vegetables and vegetable mixtures. Choice from this range depends a lot on personal taste. Some people like the texture and flavours which canning imparts; some do not.

Many of these vegetables make excellent store-cupboard material—from baked beans, sweetcorn, new potatoes and green peas to the more exotic mixtures, such as ratatouille or the Swiss-style rösti. Broad [Lima] beans, lentils and so forth are produced ready-cooked in cans, which cuts down usefully on preparation time.

Soups: there is a wider range of varieties than in dried soups, and some exotic and out-of-the ordinary flavours give an interesting lift to store-cupboard cookery. The condensed sort take up less room, and have the added advantage of making interesting 'stock' for many dishes which benefit from thick sauces.

Fish: sardines, tuna, salmon, herrings, shrimps, fish roe, anchovies (fillets or paste) and so forth.

Meat: corned and pressed beef, tongue, luncheon meat—as well as made-up dishes which range from chilli con carne to meat balls in sauce, stews and so forth. Many pâtés and meat spreads are also available canned.

Fruit: both canned and bottled (whole, in pieces, as purée or juice) sorts are useful material for many dishes. As well as the more ordinary fruits (pineapple, peaches, pears) try lychees or passion fruit pulp to serve with packet dessert mixes. Fruit juices, canned or bottled, are also very useful—apple, orange, and other varieties and blends.

Sauces and accompaniments: pickles, chutneys, sauces, relishes, jams, jellies and preserves—the range is a vast one from which to choose. All can be very tasty with spicy dishes and to serve with bought products. Vinegar (malt, wine, or cider) and oil (olive, sunflower, corn, peanut and other blends) are essential.

Herbs, spices and flavourings

No absolute list can be prepared for these additions; so much depends on personal preferences. Normally, however, the following are used on a more or less regular basis.

Cinnamon (ground or in sticks), vanilla (as pods or essence), nutmeg (preferably whole, to be grated freshly each time it is used), cloves (better whole than powdered), ginger (as dried root, powdered, preserved in syrup, or crystallized or candied). Stock cubes, pepper (ground, or as whole black or white peppercorns), curry powder, mustard (as powder, or made-up English, or French—Dijon—mustard), paprika, thyme, bay leaves, rosemary, sage, basil and tarragon.

SNACKS ON TOAST

Toast snacks have never looked so interesting, or tasted so good! These six toppings are all very quick to prepare, and each combines such intriguing flavours that they are special enough to serve as first courses, or as appetizers at parties. You might like to experiment with different breads for the toast base—rye for the Connoisseur or the Sausage and Chutney Special, and a dark brown crusty one for the Banana Fish Rafts.

Cauliflower with Béarnaise Sauce

☆ ☆   ① ·   ·

Preparation and cooking time:
25 minutes
S E R V E S 4

1 small cauliflower
1 small onion
2 tablespoons tarragon vinegar
1 tablespoon butter
1 tablespoon flour
5 fl. oz. milk
salt and pepper
1 egg yolk
4 slices of buttered toast

Chop the cauliflower finely and boil in salted water for 1½ minutes. Drain and keep warm. Peel and finely chop the onion; cook in the vinegar until the liquid is reduced to 1 tablespoonful, and strain.
Melt the butter in the saucepan, add the flour, and cook until smooth but not brown. Remove from the heat and slowly add the milk, beating all the time. Return to the heat, stirring until thickened. Remove from the heat, and beat in the strained onion and vinegar mixture and the egg yolk. Season to taste.
Spoon the cauliflower onto the butter, and milk and asparagus liquid mixture. Place the ham or bacon slices on buttered toast and grill

---

opposite: from top left: Sausage and Chutney Special, Connoisseur, Cauliflower with Béarnaise Sauce, Banana Fish Rafts, Avocado and Camembert, Open Peachburger

Banana Fish Rafts

☆   ①   ·

Preparation and cooking time:
10 minutes
S E R V E S 4

12 fish fingers [sticks]
2 tablespoons butter
2 bananas
4 slices of buttered toast
2 slices of processed or sharp Cheddar cheese

Fry the fish fingers in butter on either side until they are cooked. Peel and slice the bananas and put them on the buttered toast. Grill [broil] for about 1 minute until the bananas are softened.
Place the fish fingers on top of the sliced bananas. Cut the cheese into strips and arrange it across the fish fingers (as in the photograph) and grill [broil] until the cheese is softened. Serve at once.

Variations:
§ *Avocado and Camembert.* For 4 slices of toast peel, stone and slice 1 avocado, and dip the slices in lemon juice mixed with a little Calvados. Arrange the avocado slices on the toast, season with salt and pepper, and top with thin slices of Camembert. Grill [broil] gently and serve with chopped walnuts sprinkled on top.
§ *Open Peachburger.* For 4 slices of toast cook 4 thin hamburger steaks until they are done. Make up the Quick Chutney (or use a bought one), then place the steaks on the toast and top each with a canned peach half. Warm through on the grill [broiler] and serve each garnished with chutney.

Sausage and Chutney Special

☆   ①   ·

Preparation and cooking time:
15 minutes
S E R V E S 4

4 small pork sausages
2 teaspoons cooking oil

2 eating apples
1 large pickled gherkin
the juice of ½ lemon
3 drops Tabasco sauce
3 tablespoons milk
salt, pepper and paprika
4 slices of buttered toast
4 thin slices Cheddar cheese
8 slices of tomato

Fry the sausages in oil until cooked and golden. Meanwhile peel, core and dice the apples, and dice the gherkin. Put these into a small saucepan with the lemon juice, Tabasco, milk, salt, pepper and paprika. Simmer for 2 to 3 minutes, stirring, until the apple is tender.
Divide the mixture on to the 4 slices of toast and spread evenly. Top each with a sausage, slice of cheese and 2 slices of tomato. Grill [broil] until the cheese starts to melt, and serve immediately.

Connoisseur

☆ ☆   ① ①   ·

Preparation and cooking time:
25 minutes
S E R V E S 4

12-16 spears canned asparagus
5 fl. oz. milk
4 tablespoons flour
2 tablespoons butter
2 tablespoons cream
2 egg yolks
2 teaspoons vinegar or lemon juice
salt and cayenne pepper
4 slices of buttered toast
4 large slices ham or lean bacon

Drain the canned asparagus and add sufficient of the juice to the milk to make up to ½ pint [1¼ cups].
Make a white sauce with the flour, butter, and milk and asparagus liquid mixture. Place the ham or bacon slices on buttered toast and grill [broil] until cooked turning the bacon over once. Meanwhile beat the cream, egg yolks and vinegar into the sauce. Season with salt and cayenne pepper. Place 3-4 asparagus spears onto the cooked ham and return to the grill [broiler] to heat through.
Heat the sauce gently; do not boil or it will curdle. Serve immediately with the sauce poured over the asparagus spears.

DELICATESSEN MEALS

A local delicatessen shop has saved many of us from the consequences of forgotten shopping or empty store-cupboards. It is comparatively easy to provide a full and varied meal from 'stock', and these recipes' ingredients lists could easily be filled—partly from your own cupboard, and partly from the corner shop's shelves.

The variety of foreign sausages available now make hors d'oeuvre dishes the simplest of first courses, but many of these would also make good accompaniments to the Risotto, as would cooked meats. Or substitute these for the tuna in the Italian Salad.

below: Piquant Herrings, Risotto alla Milanese

Piquant Herrings

Preparation time:
5 minutes
SERVES 4

4 pickled herrings
1 small onion
1 sweet apple
2 teaspoons lemon juice
5 fl. oz. sour cream
salt and pepper
watercress

Drain the herrings and arrange in a serving dish. Peel and slice the onion into fine rings, cover with boiling water, and leave to soak for about 5 minutes, then drain. Cut the apple into quarters, remove the core, and peel two sections. Cut all the sections into slices and sprinkle with lemon juice. (Reserve a few of the slices with the peel on for garnish.)
Combine the rest of the apple, the onion rings, sour cream and ½ teaspoon of lemon juice; season with the salt and pepper. Spoon this over the herrings, and garnish with the reserved apple slices and watercress. Serve with brown bread and butter.

Risotto alla Milanese

Preparation and cooking time:
30 minutes
SERVES 4

1 small onion
4 tablespoons butter
8 oz. [1¼ cups] long-grain rice
5 fl. oz. white wine
1 pint [2½ cups] chicken stock
salt and pepper
good pinch of powdered saffron (optional)
2 teaspoons water
4 tablespoons grated Parmesan cheese

Peel and chop the onion finely. Melt half the butter in a saucepan and sauté the onion until tender but not browned. Add the rice, stirring until the butter has been absorbed. Add the wine, bring to the boil, and cook without the lid until the liquid is reduced by half. Add the stock, season, cover and simmer gently for about 20 minutes until all the liquid has been absorbed and the rice is tender.
Blend the saffron with the water, and stir it into the rice, mixing thoroughly with a fork. Stir in the remaining butter and the Parmesan cheese and serve immediately.

Stuffed Pancakes

Preparation and cooking time:
15 minutes
SERVES 4

4 oz. [1 cup] flour
2 eggs
½ pint [1¼ cups] milk
pinch of salt
1 pint [2½ cups] cheese sauce

Prepare the batter.
and make about eight pancakes, using a 10-inch pan.
Fill each pancake with one of the fillings suggested below, roll it up and place in a heatproof dish.
Make the cheese sauce (see page 61).
Cover all the pancakes with cheese sauce, and heat the dish in a moderate oven before serving.

Fillings:
§ Tomato sauce mixed with prawns or shrimps.
§ Chutney with sliced frankfurters.
§ Diced cooked pork with canned sauerkraut.
§ Canned spinach.

Italian Salad

Preparation time:
15 minutes
SERVES 4-6

1 lettuce
4 tomatoes
2 stalks celery
4 cooked new potatoes
8 oz. canned tuna fish, drained
black and green olives
1 tablespoon chopped anchovies
½ teaspoon dill weed or dill seed
salt and freshly ground black pepper
2 tablespoons lemon juice
4-6 tablespoons olive oil
2 tablespoons chopped parsley

Wash the lettuce, drain thoroughly, and tear the leaves into smaller pieces. Slice the tomatoes (skinned or unskinned), wash and chop celery, and slice the potatoes. Flake the tuna fish. Place these ingredients in a large bowl with the olives.
Mix the anchovies, dill, salt, pepper, lemon juice, oil and parsley. Pour these over the salad, and toss. Serve with slices of hot French bread and butter.

Frankfurter Curry

Preparation and cooking time:
30 minutes
SERVES 4

½ pint [1¼ cups] boiling water
3 tablespoons desiccated [shredded] coconut
2 lbs. tomatoes, fresh or canned
2 medium-sized onions
2 cloves of garlic
3 oz. [⅜ cup] butter
2 tablespoons curry powder
1 tablespoon flour
½ teaspoon ground ginger
salt and pepper
2 tablespoons mango chutney
4 frankfurter sausages, sliced

Pour the boiling water on to the coconut and leave to infuse. Skin and quarter the tomatoes; peel and chop the onions, peel and crush the garlic.
Melt the butter in a saucepan and sauté the onion and garlic until they are softened but not browned. Add the curry powder, flour and ginger and cook, stirring, for a few minutes.
Strain the coconut, keeping the liquid and discarding the coconut.
Add the coconut liquid with the tomatoes to the saucepan. Season with salt and pepper to taste, and simmer uncovered for 15 minutes. Add the chutney, and the sliced sausages. Reheat, and check the seasoning. Serve with plain boiled rice.

BRUNCH DISHES

below: Stuffed Baked Rolls, Grapefruit Cocktail, Bacon Bananas with Salad, Rice Salad with Red Pimiento

These dishes are ideal for many occasions, although served together, as here, they will provide an interestingly varied brunch meal that's quick and simple to prepare. The Grapefruit Cocktail would make a good first course to any meal, as well as a breakfast dish for every day. The Stuffed Baked Rolls, when served with a green salad, are a light and tasty lunch dish, while the Rice Salad could accompany rather than include cold roast meats. And the Bacon Bananas are delicious as a first course, an appetizer, or a snack meal.

Grapefruit Cocktail

☆ ① ◗

Preparation and cooking time:
10 minutes
S E R V E S 6

6 large grapefruit
castor [fine] sugar
6 maraschino cherries

Cut the grapefruit in half; squeeze the juice from half of them and remove the flesh from the other half.
Dampen the rims of 6 serving glasses with a little of the grapefruit juice and then dip these into the sugar, so that there is an even crust around the rims. To make the crust thicker, carefully dampen the rims once more with the juice and dip again in the sugar. The edges will be really crusted and frosty if the glasses are then refrigerated for a while.
Sweeten the juice and flesh of the grapefruit with sugar to taste. Put the flesh carefully into the glasses, and decorate each glass with the maraschino cherries.

Variations:
§ Sweeten the flesh of the grapefruit with a little syrup from a jar of preserved ginger, and replace the maraschino cherry with a slice of the preserved ginger.
§ Remove the flesh from all the grapefruit, replace it in six grapefruit-half skins to go under the grill [broiler]. Sprinkle each with a little rum and cover with a thin even layer of castor [fine] sugar. Just before serving place the grapefruit under the grill for about three minutes, or until the top is melted and bubbly.

Stuffed Baked Rolls

☆ ① ◗

Preparation and cooking time:
25 minutes
S E R V E S 6

4 eggs
2 oz. [½ cup] cheese, grated
1 tablespoon tomato purée
1 teaspoon made mustard
2 tablespoons cream
6 crusty rolls
2 tablespoons butter
parsley and lettuce leaves

Heat oven to 400°F (Gas Mark 6, 200°C).
Beat together the raw eggs, grated cheese, tomato purée, mustard and cream.
Cut a slice off the top of each roll, and set these 'lids' aside. Carefully remove the soft bread from the inside of the rolls—save this for making breadcrumbs for future use. Fill the rolls with the cheese mixture.
Bake in the hot oven for 10-15 minutes. Just before serving brush the lids of the rolls with a little melted butter, replace on top of the rolls, and let them heat through in the oven.
Garnish with parsley and arrange on lettuce leaves.
Serve immediately.

Variations:
§ Add a little chopped ham to the raw egg mixture before placing it inside the rolls.
§ Finely chop a few anchovy fillets and add to the mixture before placing inside the rolls—omit the mustard.

Bacon Bananas with Salad

☆ ① ◗

Preparation and cooking time:
20 minutes
S E R V E S 6

¾ lb. tomatoes
2 oranges, peeled
2 small onions, finely chopped
6 tablespoons French dressing
lettuce

6 firm bananas
mustard
freshly ground black pepper
6 thin slices of lean bacon
3 tablespoons butter
6 slices of buttered toast

Slice the tomatoes, chop the orange flesh into small pieces and add, with the finely chopped onions, to the tomatoes. Pour the French dressing over these ingredients and set aside. Arrange the salad on a serving dish with the lettuce leaves.
Peel the bananas and brush them with mustard, sprinkle with pepper and then wrap them in the bacon slices. Melt the butter in a frying pan and brown the bananas gently on all sides in the hot fat.
Put them on the slices of toast and serve with the salad.

Rice Salad with Red Pimiento

☆ ① ① ◗

Preparation and cooking time:
10 minutes
S E R V E S 6

4 oz. Emmenthal [Swiss] cheese
6 oz. [¾ cup] cold roast meat
2 pickled red peppers [pimiento]
2 medium-sized onions
1 small jar olives
5 fl. oz. plain yogurt
2 tablespoons mayonnaise
juice of ½ a lemon
salt and pepper
2 bunches watercress, chopped
8 oz. [2 cups] cooked rice

Cut the cheese into thick sticks, and the meat and red peppers into strips. Chop the onions very finely, and mix this with the halved olives and the other chopped ingredients.
Stir together with the yogurt, mayonnaise, lemon juice, salt, pepper, and chopped watercress. Mix all these ingredients together with the rice. Put into the refrigerator to chill, until ready to serve.

Variation:
If you have no cold roast meat, replace it with a few slices of lean bacon, which you have fried until crisp, and chopped up when cold.

SOUPS

If you arrive home, hungry and tired, you often need a quick warming and satisfying dish rather than a complete meal. Canned or packet soup is an obvious solution, but here we show almost equally quick ways to use foods on hand and add a few extra ingredients. It's so easy to create flavours and combinations this way which are really tasty and a little out-of-the-ordinary—such as the Senegalese Soup: a fast way to an exotic bowlful, at very little cost. Or try the Fish Soup for a truly filling meal, served with fresh crusty French bread and butter.

Pea Soup

☆ ① ① ◖

Preparation and cooking time:
10 minutes
SERVES 4

1 pint [2½ cups] **consommé**
8 oz. [1 cup] **frozen peas**
salt and pepper
2 tablespoons **sherry**

Heat the consommé very gently, add
the frozen peas and cook them until
tender. Purée in a blender or put
through a sieve. Season carefully,
add the sherry, and serve the soup
with toast or crisply fried croûtons.

Variation:
If a more substantial soup is required
add a little chopped cooked bacon
to the soup after it has been puréed.

Fish Soup

☆ ☆ ① ① ●

Preparation and cooking time:
30 minutes
SERVES 4

1 lb. **mackerel**
1½ pints [3¾ cups] **water**
parsley stalks
peppercorns
2 tablespoons **butter**
2 **leeks**
3 **carrots**
1 **turnip**
2 stalks **celery**
1 **bayleaf**
salt, pepper and thyme
chopped parsley or croûtons

Fillet the mackerel or have your
fishmonger do this for you, and place
the bones in a large saucepan with
the water, a few parsley stalks and
peppercorns. Simmer gently for a few
minutes, to make stock, while
preparing the vegetables.
Clean and cut all the vegetables into
slices. Melt the butter and gently cook
the vegetables in it, until they are
glossy but still firm. Pour the
strained stock over them; cut the
mackerel into large chunks and add
to the sliced vegetables and stock.

*opposite: above: Pea Soup
below: Fish Soup*

Add the bayleaf with the salt, pepper
and thyme. Allow to simmer a little
longer until the mackerel is cooked.
It is very important that everything
is cooked until just tender and no
more. If over-cooked the soup
ingredients break up making the dish
look unattractive and impairing the
flavour. Serve in a large soup tureen,
sprinkled with chopped parsley or
with croûtons.

Variation:
A mixture of fish may be used for
this soup. Fish which would be
suitable are rock fish [wolf-fish],
herring and red mullet.

Mushroom Soup

☆ ① ●

Preparation and cooking time:
30 minutes
SERVES 4

1 medium-sized **onion**
8 oz. **mushrooms**
4 tablespoons **butter**
4 tablespoons **flour**
15 fl. oz. [2 cups] **chicken
stock (or water and chicken
stock cube)**
5 fl. oz. **milk**
1 tablespoon **chopped parsley**
2½ fl. oz. single [light] **cream**
salt and pepper

Peel and finely chop the onion; wash
and slice the mushrooms. Melt the
butter in a saucepan and sauté the
onion until soft but not brown. Add
the mushrooms and flour and sauté for
5 minutes. Remove from the heat
and stir in the stock, adding slowly
at first and stirring all the time.
Return to the heat and bring to
boiling point, stirring until it has
thickened. Blend in the milk, and add
most of the parsley, saving a little for
a garnish. Purée in a blender until
smooth. Return to the saucepan,
re-heat, and season with salt and
pepper to taste.
Just before serving remove from the
heat and stir in the cream. Sprinkle
each bowl with chopped parsley.

Note: An alternative garnish would
be to save some slices of mushroom
and garnish with those before serving.
If a chunky soup is preferred then
do not purée in the blender, and
stir in all the parsley.

Tomato Soup

☆ ① ◖

Preparation and cooking time:
10 minutes
SERVES 4

1 medium-sized **onion**
2 tablespoons **butter**
4 tablespoons **flour**
½ pint [1¼ cups] **milk**
½ pint [1¼ cups] **water**
4 tablespoons **canned tomato purée**
1 teaspoon **sugar**
pinch of dried mixed herbs
salt and pepper

Peel and finely chop the onion.
Melt the butter in medium-sized
saucepan and cook the onion in it
until tender but not coloured. Add
the flour, and cook until the mixture
is thick but not brown. Remove from
heat and gradually stir in the milk
and water, beating until smooth. Stir
in the tomato purée, sugar and dried
herbs. Season with salt and pepper to
taste, and simmer for about 6-7
minutes or until the onion is cooked.
If you prefer, put the soup in the
blender for a few seconds. Serve with
chopped parsley or fried croûtons on
top.

Senegalese Soup

☆ ① ◖

Preparation and cooking time:
5 minutes
SERVES 4

About 15 fl. oz. [2 cups]
canned beef consommé
3 oz. [6 tablespoons] **cream cheese**
¾ teaspoon **curry powder**

Add sufficient water to the consommé
to make it up to 1 pint [2½ cups].
Pour into blender, add remaining
ingredients, and blend until smooth.
Return to the saucepan and heat,
then serve.

Note: Add an extra ¼ teaspoon of
curry powder if you like extra hot
foods.

73

STUFFED VEGETABLES

One of the best ways of quickly adding interest to a meal is to serve stuffed vegetables with it—as a first course or appetizer, as a separate vegetable course, or as an accompaniment within the main course. They look most attractive, and often add a new and spicy flavour to a familiar food. Stuffed vegetables may also be served very successfully at parties, for they are easy to prepare, often inexpensive and make ideal 'snack' food. Stuffed Tomatoes, hot or cold, are always popular—and for a change try the Stuffed Chicory [Endive] or the Mushrooms.

Stuffed Mushrooms

☆ ① ♨

Preparation and cooking time:
30 minutes
SERVES 4

12 large mushrooms
1 small onion
2 tablespoons butter
6 tablespoons fresh breadcrumbs
1 tablespoon chopped parsley
1 teaspoon tomato purée
salt and freshly ground black
    pepper
2 egg yolks
For the cheese sauce:
2 tablespoons butter
4 tablespoons flour
½ pint [1¼ cups] milk
salt, pepper and a pinch of dry
    mustard
2 oz. [½ cup] grated cheese

Heat oven to 375°F (Gas Mark 5,
190°C).
Wash and peel the mushrooms.
Remove the stalks and chop them,
with four of the mushroom caps.
Peel and chop the onion finely. Melt
the butter and gently fry the onion.
Add the chopped mushrooms and
stalks, breadcrumbs, parsley, tomato
purée and salt and pepper. Remove
the pan from the heat and mix the egg
yolks into the mixture to bind it
together. Fill the remaining whole
mushroom caps with this mixture and
arrange them in a buttered heatproof
dish.
Melt the butter for the sauce, remove
from the heat and add the flour. Blend
it well into the butter and gradually add
the milk. Return the pan to the heat
and bring the sauce to the boil stirring
all the time. Season it with salt, pepper
and mustard, and add the grated
cheese, reserving a little for the top.
Cook a little longer until the cheese
has melted and the sauce is of a
coating consistency.
Coat the mushrooms with the cheese
sauce, sprinkle with a little extra
grated cheese, and bake for 15 minutes.

Variations:
§ Fill the mushrooms with 2
tablespoons crumbled blue cheese
mixed with the fried onion and
mushroom stalks and 2 tablespoons of
breadcrumbs. Pour melted butter over

*opposite: top: Stuffed Tomatoes
left: Stuffed Aubergines*

each mushroom. Bake for about 15
minutes.
§ Fill the mushrooms with 6 slices of
finely chopped bacon cooked until
crisp, added to the chopped mushroom.
Mix this with a tablespoon of tomato
pickle or chutney and sprinkle with 2
tablespoons of fresh breadcrumbs.
Pour a little melted butter over each
one and bake for about 15 minutes.

Stuffed Peppers

☆ ☆ ① ① ♨

Preparation and cooking time:
30 minutes
SERVES 6

6 green peppers
For the stuffing:
1 onion
4 oz. [1 cup] mushrooms
2 tablespoons butter
4 tomatoes
6 oz. [1½ cups] cooked brown rice
salt and pepper
chopped fresh thyme and parsley
½ pint [1¼ cups] stock

Heat oven to 350°F (Gas Mark 4,
180°C).
Cut a slice from the stem end of each
pepper. Scoop out the seeds and core.
Parboil the peppers in boiling water
for five minutes, drain and refresh
them under cold water. Set aside. Peel
and chop the onion and slice the
mushrooms. Fry the onion in the
melted butter until it is soft but not
brown and add the mushrooms to it.
Peel and dice the tomatoes, and add
them to the pan with the onion
mixture. Add the cooked rice and
season carefully with salt, pepper and
herbs.
Stuff the peppers with this mixture
and pack them into a well buttered,
deep heatproof dish. Carefully spoon
over the stock. Cook for about 20
minutes in the oven, basting frequently.

Variations:
§ In place of the stock spoon a good
tomato sauce or half a pint [1¼ cups]
of tomato soup over the peppers.
§ Replace the four tomatoes with 6
ounces [¾ cup] of shredded cooked
ham, and add a little finely chopped
garlic or garlic salt to the onions in the
pan.
§ Any chopped, left-over meat may be
used as the main ingredient.

Stuffed Chicory

☆ ☆ ① ♨

Preparation and cooking time:
30 minutes
SERVES 4

4 large heads of chicory [endive]
2 tablespoons butter
1 small onion, finely chopped
2 tablespoons flour
5 fl. oz. stock
4 oz. [½ cup] canned tuna or salmon
1 teaspoon chopped parsley
salt and pepper
melted butter and dry breadcrumbs

Heat oven to 375°F (Gas Mark 5,
190°C).
Remove any discoloured leaves and
wash the chicory. Cut each head in half
lengthwise, and remove the centre
leaves—these are ideal for a salad.
Melt the butter and soften the finely
chopped onion in it. Remove from
the heat and stir in the flour and the
stock. Bring the sauce to the boil and
continue to cook until thickened. Add
the drained flaked fish and chopped
parsley, and season with salt and
pepper.
Arrange the chicory heads in a well
buttered heatproof dish and fill them
with the fish mixture. Scatter with
breadcrumbs and spoon melted butter
over the chicory. Pour a little water or
stock into the base of the dish.
Bake for about 20 minutes. If the tops
of the chicory become too brown,
cover them with a piece of aluminium
foil.

Stuffed Tomatoes

☆ ① ♨

Preparation and cooking time:
20 minutes
SERVES 4

1 medium-sized onion
1 green pepper
1 tablespoon butter
8 oz. [1 cup] sweet corn
8 large tomatoes
salt and paprika pepper
grated Parmesan cheese

Heat oven to 375°F (Gas Mark 5,
190°C).
Chop the onion; slice and chop the
green pepper. Melt the butter and

gently sauté the onion and pepper in it. Add the corn and heat through. Cut the tops from the tomatoes, scoop out the centres and add these to the corn mixture. Season the mixture with salt and paprika and stuff the tomatoes with it. Sprinkle a little grated Parmesan cheese over the tomatoes and place in an ovenproof dish. Bake for 10 minutes.

Variation:
Mushroom stuffed tomatoes. Heat oven to 325°F (Gas Mark 3, 170°C). Add 4 large chopped and sautéed mushrooms to the tomato pulp with a tablespoon of breadcrumbs, and season the mixture well with salt, pepper and a pinch of dried basil. Place a teaspoonful of this mixture into each tomato. Arrange the tomato cases in a casserole. Break an egg into each tomato. Season with a little salt and pepper. Cook in the oven until the eggs are set—about 15 minutes.

Cold Stuffed Tomatoes

☆　　①①　　◗

Preparation and cooking time:
10 minutes
SERVES 4

8 large tomatoes
8 oz. [1 cup] cottage cheese
½ teaspoon curry powder
8 sprigs of parsley
salt
4 oz. prawns or shrimps

Cut the tops from the tomatoes, and trim the bases if necessary so that they will sit securely on the serving dish. Scoop out the centres with a teaspoon. Leave the tomatoes upside down to drain while mixing the filling together. Season the cottage cheese with the curry powder and salt, and fold in the prawns or shrimps. Fill the prepared tomatoes generously with this mixture. Replace the tomato cap on top of the tomato at an angle. Decorate with a sprig of parsley.
This dish would be very suitable to start a meal—in which case one tomato each would be sufficient. Cold stuffed tomatoes are also excellent for those counting calories.

Variations:
§ Finely dice a few chunks of

cucumber. Season with salt and pepper and a little freshly chopped mint. Fold into a few tablespoons of sour cream, and spoon into the tomato cases.
§ Cook a few new potatoes and, while still warm, dice and toss in a well seasoned vinaigrette dressing with chopped parsley. Or when they are cold mix into a mayonnaise with chopped gherkins or capers.

Stuffed Aubergines

☆ ☆　　①①　　◉

Preparation and cooking time:
30 minutes
SERVES 4

2 medium-sized aubergines [eggplants]
1 large onion, sliced
1 large clove of garlic chopped
6 canned tomatoes, chopped
4 tablespoons vegetable oil
salt and freshly ground black pepper
a large pinch of dried marjoram
1 teaspoon chopped parsley
3 tablespoons fresh breadcrumbs
2 tablespoons butter

Heat oven to 375°F (Gas Mark 5, 190°C).
Wipe the aubergines. Cut each in half lengthwise and, using a metal spoon, carefully remove the pulp. Sprinkle a little salt inside the aubergine cases and turn them upside down to drain—this will remove excess water from the shells.
Heat the oil and gently cook the sliced onion and chopped garlic. Chop the pulp from the aubergines; add this to the onion and garlic, with the chopped tomatoes. Cook a little longer, then season with the salt, pepper and herbs, and add the breadcrumbs.
Drain and wipe the aubergine shells and spoon in the filling. Dot the butter over, and bake for about 20 minutes.

Variations:
Prepare the aubergines as above, and try an alternative filling, mixed with the aubergine pulp.
§ ½ pound of minced [ground] beef fried with a finely chopped onion, a tablespoon of tomato purée and seasoned well. Bind the mixture

together with a beaten egg.
§ ½ pound of minced [ground] beef fried with a finely chopped onion, and seasoned with ¼ teaspoon chilli powder, a little salt and a tablespoon of chutney or pickle.

Stuffed Baked Potatoes

☆　　①　　●

Preparation and cooking time:
45 minutes
SERVES 4

8 small potatoes
a little oil
salt
4 tablespoons butter
2 oz. [½ cup] strong cheese, grated
2½ fl. oz. sour cream
2 tablespoons chopped spring onions [scallions] or chives
6 slices streaky bacon, fried until crisp

Heat oven to 425°F (Gas Mark 7, 220°C).
Choose firm smooth potatoes: new potatoes are not suitable for baking. It is also best to choose similarly sized potatoes to ensure even cooking. Wash, scrub and dry the potatoes, and prick them all over with a fork. Rub a little oil into the skins, roll them in salt, and bake in the oven until cooked.
When the potatoes are cooked, cut them in half, scoop out the insides, and mix with the butter, cheese, sour cream and chopped spring onions or chives. Refill the potato shells and return to the oven to reheat thoroughly Chop the bacon into small pieces and sprinkle over the potatoes before serving.

Variations:
§ A small bunch of watercress, chopped and mixed with a little cream cheese, salt, and freshly ground black pepper.
§ Coarsely chopped celery mixed with the cooked flesh of the potato, and a little melted butter mixed into it.
§ Chopped red pepper with a pinch of marjoram mixed into the flesh of the potato with a little butter.

opposite: Stuffed Peppers

76

QUICK VEGETABLE DISHES

left: Summer Vegetable Medley
below: Glazed Carrots, Cauliflower à la Polonaise, French Beans with Tomatoes

When cooking time is at a premium the most sensible vegetables often seem to be the ones straight from the freezer, or from cans. While these are sometimes the easiest solution, they are by no means the only answer to your problem. Pre-packaged vegetables are often rather boring—so if you do serve them try adding a white or cheese sauce, or mix packets to give the appearance and taste a lift. But best of all try the recipes here—any may be prepared while the main dish is cooking, and all provide a fresh approach to the often neglected subject of vegetable cookery.

Glazed Carrots

☆ ① ◑

Preparation and cooking time:
20 minutes
S E R V E S 4

10 medium-sized carrots
2 tablespoons water
2 tablespoons butter
pinch of sugar
salt and freshly ground black
　pepper
a little chopped parsley

Thinly peel the carrots and cut them diagonally into thick chunks. Heat the water and butter in a heavy saucepan and add the pinch of sugar. Put the sliced carrots into the pan and simmer them gently, covered with a tightly fitting lid. Allow the water to evaporate completely—taking care not to overcook the carrots. They are left lightly glazed by the butter. Finish with a little extra butter and salt, and pepper, and sprinkle with the chopped parsley.

French Beans with Tomatoes

☆ ① ◑

Preparation and cooking time:
20 minutes
S E R V E S 4

4 tomatoes
1 lb. prepared fresh or frozen
　French beans
3 tablespoons butter
salt and freshly ground black pepper
chopped parsley

Peel and dice the tomatoes. Cook the beans in boiling salted water; drain thoroughly and turn into a warm serving dish. Melt the butter in a shallow pan and quickly sauté the diced tomato in it. Add the salt, pepper, and parsley to the tomato mixture and pour it over the beans.

Variations:
§ *French Beans with Onion.* Prepare and boil 1 pound of French beans. Drain them very well and turn into a warm serving dish. Chop a medium-sized onion finely. Heat 2 tablespoons of butter in a pan and add the finely chopped onion. Fry slowly until golden brown, taking care not to burn it. Add salt and pepper to the onion and spoon the mixture over the beans.
§ French beans may also be served as a salad: leaving them whole if possible, cook until just tender. Season them with a mixture of a little lemon juice and oil, plenty of black pepper and a little salt.

Summer Vegetable Medley

☆ ☆ ① ◑

Preparation and cooking time:
30 minutes
S E R V E S 4

1 small green cabbage
½ lb. green beans
1 lb. new potatoes
3 small onions
½ lb. small carrots
salt and freshly ground black
　pepper
freshly chopped mint or thyme
hot chicken stock or water
2 tablespoons butter

Remove the outer leaves of the cabbage. Cut it into about six chunks, leaving the stem on so that the leaves stay together; wash thoroughly.
Prepare and cut the green beans into even lengths. Scrape the new potatoes and cut them in half. Peel the onions and cut into even-sized slices. Separate the slices into rings. Scrape the carrots and cut them lengthwise into similar lengths as the beans. Place all the vegetables in a large saucepan. Season with salt, pepper and a little chopped mint or thyme.
Pour over enough hot stock or

water to half-cover up the vegetables. Dot them with the butter. Cover the pan with a tight-fitting lid and simmer for 15-20 minutes or until the vegetables are just tender. Serve with cold or roast meat.

Note: It is essential that all the vegetables are cut into even-sized pieces to ensure that all the vegetables are tender at the same time.

Variation:
A few peeled and quartered tomatoes may be added to the pan when the vegetables are cooked. This would add a little new colour to the finished dish.

Cauliflower à la Polonaise

☆ ☆ ① ●

Preparation and cooking time:
25 to 30 minutes, excluding soaking time
S E R V E S 4

1 medium-sized cauliflower
For the sauce:
2 tablespoons butter
4 tablespoons fresh breadcrumbs
juice of ½ a lemon
1 chopped hard-boiled egg
2 tablespoons chopped parsley
salt and freshly ground black
　pepper

Remove one or two outside leaves from the bottom of the stalk of the cauliflower, and trim the stalk parallel with the base of the cauliflower. Leave it to soak in cold salt water for about half an hour, then cook in boiling water for about 20 minutes. Test it by inserting the point of a sharp knife into the stem; it is cooked if the knife can be easily inserted. Drain it well and place on a warm serving dish.
To make the sauce, melt the butter in a heavy frying pan. Add the breadcrumbs and fry them until golden. Remove from the heat to ensure they do not continue browning. Add the lemon juice, chopped hard-boiled egg, chopped parsley, salt and pepper. Mix the mixture over a gentle heat, combining all the ingredients well.
Spoon the sauce over the cauliflower and serve. This dish is excellent served with roast or cold meats, or it can be served as a separate vegetable dish.

SUPER SALADS

Made with care and presented attractively, a really tasty salad is one of the best quick dishes possible—it can stand alone as a first or other separate course, or combine with cold meats as a main dish. These recipes use vegetables, fruits and other ingredients in interesting ways which give the individual flavours a lift—yet all are simple to prepare, and none requires an especially expensive ingredient. You could always add your own flavours to those we have suggested, or substitute others to taste.

Deluxe Potato Salad

☆☆   ①   ◑

Preparation and cooking time:
25 minutes
SERVES 4

1½ lbs. potatoes
1 tablespoon chopped onion
2 tablespoons wine or malt vinegar
4 celery stalks
about 8 green olives
1 tablespoon chopped canned red pimiento
salt and pepper
5 fl. oz. mayonnaise (see page 61)

Peel the potatoes and boil in salted water for about 15 minutes or until cooked; drain, and allow to cool enough so that they can be handled. Dice, and mix with the chopped onion and vinegar while still fairly hot. Cut the celery in fine slices. Remove the stones [pits] from olives and slice, then mix together the potato mixture with the celery, olives and pimiento. Add salt and pepper to taste. Spoon over the mayonnaise, and toss lightly.

Variations:
§ To make a plainer potato salad omit the celery, olives and pimiento.
§ To make this recipe more substantial, add 7 ounces of canned flaked tuna fish to it, and serve with rye bread and butter.
§ For a party serve on a bed of lettuce and put a few whole olives on the top for decoration.

Smoked Salmon Salad

☆☆   ①①①◑

Preparation time:
10 minutes
SERVES 4

4 oz. thinly sliced smoked salmon
2 pickled gherkins or cucumbers
about ½ lb. canned pineapple pieces
2 tablespoons sweet corn
2 tablespoons chopped parsley
1 tablespoon chives
5 fl. oz. yogurt
2 tablespoons lemon juice
salt and pepper
¼ teaspoon dry mustard

Cut the salmon into thin strips, and roll each strip up. Chop the gherkins, and drain the pineapple pieces (the juice is not used in this recipe). Arrange layers of salmon rolls, gherkin, pineapple pieces and sweet corn, and top with the chopped parsley and chives, as in the photograph.
Mix together the remaining ingredients and pour over the arranged salad just before serving. Serve with thickly cut brown bread and butter.

Iceberg Salad

☆   ①   ◑

Preparation and cooking time:
15 minutes
SERVES 4

4 eggs
1 head Webb's Wonder [iceberg] lettuce
1 box cress
2 lemons
salt and pepper

1 teaspoon sugar
3 tablespoons olive oil

Put the eggs in a small saucepan, cover with water, and boil for about 10 minutes. Drain, and cool in cold water.
While the eggs are boiling wash the lettuce and drain thoroughly. Trim the roots off the cress, wash and drain well. Squeeze the lemons and mix the juice thoroughly with the salt, pepper, sugar and oil. Tear the lettuce into serving pieces, and arrange them in a bowl with the cress.
Pour on most of the lemon and vinegar mixture, and toss well. Peel and slice the eggs, arrange them carefully in the salad, and pour the rest of the dressing over them. If the eggs are tossed with the salad they will break and would not look so attractive.

Variations:
§ Omit the cress and use a bunch of watercress.
§ To make a more substantial salad add julienne strips of mild cheese, ham, beef or chicken. If chicken is used then the dressing could be slowly added to 2 tablespoons of yogurt and, for a change, could even be curry flavoured.

Sauerkraut Salad

☆ ① ◗

Preparation time:
10 minutes
SERVES 4

2 green apples
4 tablespoons wine vinegar
2 carrots
approximately 8 oz. canned
    sauerkraut
3 tablespoons olive oil
salt and pepper
1 tablespoon sugar
few sprigs of fresh dill (or 1 teaspoon
dried dill weed or dried dill seed)

Peel and core the apples. Grate them,
and spoon over a little of the wine
vinegar to prevent the apple from
turning brown. Peel, trim and grate
the carrots, and combine the apple,
carrots and sauerkraut. Mix together
the remaining vinegar, oil, salt, pepper,
sugar and dill.
Pour the dressing over the combined
ingredients and toss well. This would
be delicious with hot or cold sausages
of any kind or with sliced salami.

Mexican Melon Salad

☆ ☆ ① ① ◗

Preparation and cooking time:
15 minutes
SERVES 4

approximately ½ lb. mixed frozen
    vegetables, including sweet corn,
    peas and red pimiento
2 pears
3 tablespoons lemon juice
½ a watermelon
4 tablespoons olive oil
salt
pinch of sugar
dash of chilli powder (or to taste)
dash of Worcestershire sauce
1 tablespoon chopped parsley
    (optional)

Cook the frozen vegetables in boiling
salted water for about 3-4 minutes, or
until they are cooked but not mushy,
drain, and allow to cool. Peel and core
the pears and cut into pieces. Pour
the lemon juice over the pears, to
prevent their going brown. Scoop
flesh out of the watermelon in ball
shapes. If you do not have the cutter

to make balls, cut the melon into cubes,
removing the black seeds.
Drain the lemon juice off the pears
and make the dressing by combining
it with oil, salt, sugar, chilli,
Worcestershire sauce and chopped
parsley. Combine the vegetables,
pears and melon, pour over the
dressing, and toss gently.
This salad is particularly good with
cold baked ham.

Note: When preparing salad using
melon, it should be remembered that
once the melon is mixed with the
ingredients it should be used
reasonably quickly as the melon makes
extra water, and so would dilute the
flavour of the dressing. If you want to
prepare this salad early keep the melon
balls separate, and drain them well
before combining them with the
other ingredients.

*below: Iceberg Salad, Mexican Melon
Salad, Sauerkraut Salad, Smoked
Salmon Salad*

WAYS WITH CORN

Corn is always a popular and attractive vegetable, whether served fresh on the cob, or at other times of the year from cans or frozen packets. But too often its versatility is ignored, and it is sadly relegated to appear as a plain accompanying vegetable. Here we have provided recipes which allow corn its own role—in a soufflé, a chowder and a crunchy bake, as well as a deliciously simple first course.

Broiled Corn

Preparation and cooking time:
10 minutes
SERVES 2

2 ears of corn on the cob—frozen
  or fresh
2 tablespoons butter
salt and freshly ground black pepper

Boil the husked corn cobs in salted water until it is tender. Drain them well. Melt the butter and brush it over the corn. Sprinkle with pepper and salt. Grill [broil] until golden, turning the corn from time to time. The corn may be cooked under a grill [broiler] or over charcoal.

Corn Soufflé

Preparation and cooking time:
40 minutes
SERVES 4

3 tablespoons butter
3 tablespoons flour
8 fl. oz. [1 cup] milk
8 oz. [1 cup] cooked corn
salt, pepper and ¼ teaspoon
  mustard

4 oz. [1 cup] grated cheese
3 eggs, separated

Heat oven to 350°F (Gas Mark 4, 180°C).
Butter a 2½-pint soufflé or pie dish. Melt the butter in a saucepan. Remove from the heat and stir in the flour. Gradually blend in the milk, return to the heat, and bring to the boil, stirring constantly.
Cook until the sauce is thickened and smooth. Add the cooked corn, salt, pepper, mustard and most of the cheese; allow to cool slightly. Stir the egg yolks into the sauce, one at a time. Beat the egg whites until stiff, and gently fold into the corn mixture. Pour it into the prepared dish. Sprinkle with the remaining cheese and bake for 20-30 minutes until well risen and golden brown on top.
Serve immediately.

Corn Chowder

Preparation and cooking time:
25 minutes
SERVES 4

2 medium-sized potatoes
1 medium-sized onion
1 tablespoon butter
3 tablespoons chopped bacon
8 oz. [1 cup] cooked corn
8 canned tomatoes
salt, pepper and thyme
1¼ pints [3 cups] stock

Peel and dice the potatoes. Peel and slice the onion. Melt the butter in a saucepan and gently soften the onion and bacon in it. Cook until they begin to brown. Add the potato, corn and tomatoes to the pan with the seasonings. Pour in the stock and bring to the boil. Cover and simmer the chowder for about 15 minutes or until the potato is cooked.

Variations:
§ Sprinkle a little grated cheese over the corn chowder just before serving.
§ Serve hot herb or anchovy bread with the chowder. Cut a long French loaf into slices to within ½-inch from the bottom. Do not cut right through. Mix a few mixed chopped herbs or anchovy paste with enough butter to cover the top and each side of the slices. Spread the flavoured butter on each side of the slices, press together again, and spread the remaining butter over the sides and top. Wrap in foil, and place in a hot oven until heated through and crisp all over.

Corn Bake

Preparation and cooking time:
25 minutes
SERVES 4

½ a green pepper
1 medium-sized onion
3 tablespoons butter
2 tablespoons flour
1 teaspoon made mustard
8 fl. oz. [1 cup] milk
4 tomatoes, peeled and quartered
8 oz. [1 cup] cooked corn
1 teaspoon Worcestershire sauce
2 hard-boiled eggs, sliced
a little melted butter and
  breadcrumbs

Heat oven to 400°F (Gas Mark 6, 200°C).
Slice the green pepper and onion. Melt the butter and soften the vegetables in it. Add the flour and mustard and stir well. Remove from the heat and gradually add the milk. Return to the heat and bring to the boil, stirring constantly. Add the tomatoes, corn and Worcestershire sauce. Turn into a heatproof dish, top with slices of hard boiled egg and finally scatter breadcrumbs on the top, spooning a little melted butter over all.
Bake for about 10-15 minutes until the Corn Bake is bubbling.

---

opposite: back: Corn Fritters, Corn Chowder, Corn Soufflé front: Broiled Corn

PANCAKES AND BLINI

Once you have learned just how easy a pancake batter is to prepare, you will enjoy making and serving these delicious recipes. Or try the Potato and Bacon Pancakes, which do not use batter at all! The fillings may be varied almost indefinitely to suit your taste and pocket, and to dress the dish up to party standards or down to a simple one-course meal. The recipes here are all savoury ones, but you could always provide a fruit purée filling instead—for speed this could be from a can, or seasonal fresh fruit, lightly stewed.

Potato and Bacon Pancakes

☆ ☆ ① 🍶

Preparation and cooking time:
15 minutes
SERVES 4

3 slices bacon, chopped
4 medium-sized potatoes
salt and freshly ground black
  pepper
1 tablespoon fresh chives, chopped
2 tablespoons vegetable oil
2 tablespoons butter

Gently fry the chopped bacon in its
own fat. Peel the potatoes and grate
them on a coarse grater into a large
bowl. Season with salt and pepper and
add the chives and bacon to the
potatoes. Work quickly so that the
potatoes do not discolour.
Melt the butter and oil in a heavy-
based pancake or omelette pan. The
fat must be hot, but take care not
to let it burn. Using about 2
tablespoons of mixture at a time, fry
the pancakes, flattening them well with
a spatula, while they are cooking. Fry
on each side until they are crisp and
golden.
Serve at once.

Cheese and Ham Pancakes

☆ ☆ ① ① 🍶

Preparation and cooking time:
30 minutes
SERVES 4

4 oz. [1 cup] flour
salt and cayenne pepper
2 eggs
1 tablespoon melted butter
1 oz. [4 tablespoons] grated Gruyère
  [Swiss] cheese
7-10 fl. oz. [1-1¼ cups] milk and
  water mixed
½ pint [1¼ cups] white sauce (see
  page 61)
½ lb. chopped lean cooked ham
melted butter

---

opposite: top: Blini
below: Finnish Spinach Pancakes

Heat oven to 400°F (Gas Mark 6,
200°C).
Make the pancake batter (see page
62), adding the cayenne pepper with
the flour and salt. Add the cheese, and
set aside, while making the sauce (see
page 61). Cook the sauce for a few
minutes, add the chopped ham and
set aside. Heat the pancake pan, add a
little oil, and when hot drop in a few
spoonfuls of pancake mixture—these
pancakes should be fairly thin. Cook
for about 2 minutes on each side or
until brown. If the batter is too thick,
add more of the liquid.
Stuff each pancake with a large
spoonful of the filling, roll up and
arrange them in a buttered heatproof
dish. Spoon over the melted
butter. Brown well in the oven,
for about 10 minutes.

Finnish Spinach Pancakes

☆ ☆ ① 🍶

Preparation and cooking time:
20 minutes
MAKES about 12 pancakes

4 oz. [1 cup] flour
½ teaspoon salt
¼ teaspoon grated nutmeg
2 eggs
½ pt. [1¼ cups] milk
1 tablespoon melted butter
4 oz. [½ cup] cooked spinach

Make the pancake batter (see page 62),
adding the nutmeg with the flour and
salt. Set it aside while preparing the
spinach.
Squeeze the freshly cooked spinach
between two plates, until it is very dry
and then chop it finely. Add it to the
batter.
Heat a heavy based pancake pan and
wipe it over with oil or a little melted
butter. This is to prevent the pancake
from sticking; not to fry it. When the
pan is hot drop 1 or 2 tablespoonfuls
of batter into it—tipping the pan to
spread the mixture evenly. Cook for
2 to 3 minutes, and with a spoon or
spatula turn the pancake over to cook
a further 2 to 3 minutes, or until it has
browned slightly. Pile the pancakes on
top of one another on a heated dish,
covered with a clean cloth or
aluminium foil to keep them warm.
Oil the pan again if necessary, and
finish cooking the pancakes.

Serve the spinach pancakes as a
vegetable course with cranberry sauce
or loganberries.

Blini

☆ ☆ ☆ ①

Preparation and cooking time:
about 40 minutes
MAKES about 30 blinis

1 pint [2½ cups] milk
½ tablespoon dried yeast, or
  ½ oz. fresh baker's yeast
½ teaspoon castor [fine] sugar
  (for use with dried yeast)
8 oz. [2 cups] wholewheat flour
8 oz. [2 cups] flour
½ teaspoon salt
2 tablespoons melted butter
2 eggs, separated

Accompaniments: caviar, lumpfish roe
or smoked roe, sour cream, chopped
onions (vary the quantities according
to your taste).
Heat half the milk until lukewarm
and dissolve the yeast in it. If you are
using dried yeast, dissolve the sugar in
the lukewarm milk and sprinkle the
dried yeast on top. Leave it until it is
frothy. Add half of the flours and
allow the dough to rise, covered, in a
warm place for about 25 minutes, until
risen. Add the remaining flour and
milk with the salt, melted butter, and
the egg yolks. Fold in the egg whites,
stiffly beaten.
Heat a small well-oiled pancake pan or
griddle, and add a tablespoonful of
the mixture to the pan, tipping the
pan so that the mixture spreads a
little. Cook on both sides until brown
and risen. The blinis should be thin
and full of holes. If the batter seems too
thick a little more warm milk may be
carefully added. Keep the first blinis
in a warm dish while frying the others.
To serve, spread with butter or sour
cream (or both) and stack one on top
of the other. They should be folded
over or rolled and eaten hot with the
accompaniments. These are sufficiently
filling to be served as a main course,
perhaps starting the meal with a clear
soup.

85

OMELETTES

Eggs are just about the most versatile of all foods, and an omelette is perhaps the quickest way of turning them into an attractive dish that can make a satisfying meal. On page 62 we give a recipe for a plain omelette with variations to add interesting. extra flavours, and here a delicious French Omelette, and some really unusual ways in which to serve soufflé (or fluffy) omelettes.

Remember that a perfect omelette cooks very quickly—the whole operation must not take more than a few minutes. Never try to cook too large an omelette at once—it's much better to take the extra time to make two or three.

Omelette Provençale

☆ ☆   ① ☽

Preparation and cooking time:
15 minutes
S E R V E S 4

8 eggs
salt and freshly ground black
    pepper
2 tablespoons water
4 tablespoons butter
For the filling:
1 medium onion
2 tablespoons butter
8 large tomatoes
basil, oregano and parsley
salt and pepper

Prepare the filling first. Peel and finely slice the onion and gently sauté it in the melted butter. Peel and chop the tomatoes. Add these to the onion and simmer for about 10 minutes. Season with the chopped herbs, salt and pepper.
Set the pan to one side of the stove, where the mixture will be kept hot. Now make the omelettes.
Break four of the eggs at a time into a bowl. Season with salt and pepper and add 1 tablespoon of water. Melt half of the butter in an omelette pan and pour the beaten eggs on to it.
Start cooking, at a very high temperature, then reduce the heat a little. To prevent the omelette sticking to the pan shake the pan to and fro while cooking keeping the egg mixture moving with a fork. While the omelette is still 'runny' in the centre, add half of the tomato and onion filling.
Cook until the egg mixture is fairly firm and serve immediately.
Repeat the whole process with the remaining four eggs.

Fluffy Omelette

with Orange and Camembert filling

☆ ☆   ① ①   ☽

Preparation and cooking time:
10 minutes
S E R V E S 2

3 eggs, separated
salt and pepper
4 tablespoons milk or single [light]
    cream
2 tablespoons butter
2 oz. Camembert, sliced
6 oz. [¾ cup] canned mandarin
    orange segments

Beat the egg yolks with a little salt and pepper to taste; add the milk or cream. Beat the egg whites until stiff, and fold lightly into the egg yolk mixture. Heat the butter in a pan, pour in the mixture, and cook over a low heat until it is set and golden brown underneath.
Transfer the pan to the preheated grill [broiler] and put under the heat until it just starts to brown. Place the slices of Camembert and the oranges on top and return to the grill [broiler] until heated through. Fold over and serve immediately.

Variations: When the top of the omelette is beginning to brown omit the oranges and Camembert and fill with one of the following:
§ *Pimiento:* Cut one green and one red pepper in half and remove seeds and white pith. Slice them finely and sauté in 1 tablespoon of butter. Add 4 tablespoons of water and simmer until tender.
§ *Swiss Gruyère:* Fry 1 teaspoon chopped onion in about 2 teaspoons butter until it is tender. Cut about 2 ounces of Gruyère [Swiss] cheese into slices and fold the cheese and onion into the omelette mixture before cooking.

Soufflé Omelette

with Chinese Gooseberries

☆ ☆   ① ① ① ☽

Preparation and cooking time:
10 minutes
S E R V E S 2

3 Chinese gooseberries
3 eggs, separated
1 tablespoon castor [fine] sugar
3 tablespoons milk or water
1 tablespoon butter
a little extra castor [fine] sugar

Remove the skin from the Chinese gooseberries and slice them. Whisk the egg whites until fluffy. Beat the yolks separately, add the sugar and milk or water, and fold the egg whites into the egg yolk mixture.
Heat the butter in a frying pan until foaming but not browned, and pour in the mixture. Smooth it over and cook until golden brown underneath. Brown the top under the grill [broiler]. Loosen the omelette and arrange the fruit on one half, fold over the other half of omelette and slide it on to a warmed plate. Just before serving sprinkle with a little extra castor [fine] sugar.

Variations:
§ *Peaches and Brandy:* Heat sliced peaches (fresh or canned) in a little brandy. Spoon on to the omelette, dust with cinnamon, fold, and sprinkle with cinnamon and castor [fine] sugar.
§ *Apples and sour cream:* Grate a large peeled eating apple and stir in a few chopped walnuts. Add 2-3 tablespoons of sour cream, spoon into omelette, fold, and serve immediately.

---

opposite: top: Soufflé and Fluffy Omelettes with Chinese Gooseberry filling, Orange and Camembert filling Pimiento filling
below: Omelette Provençale

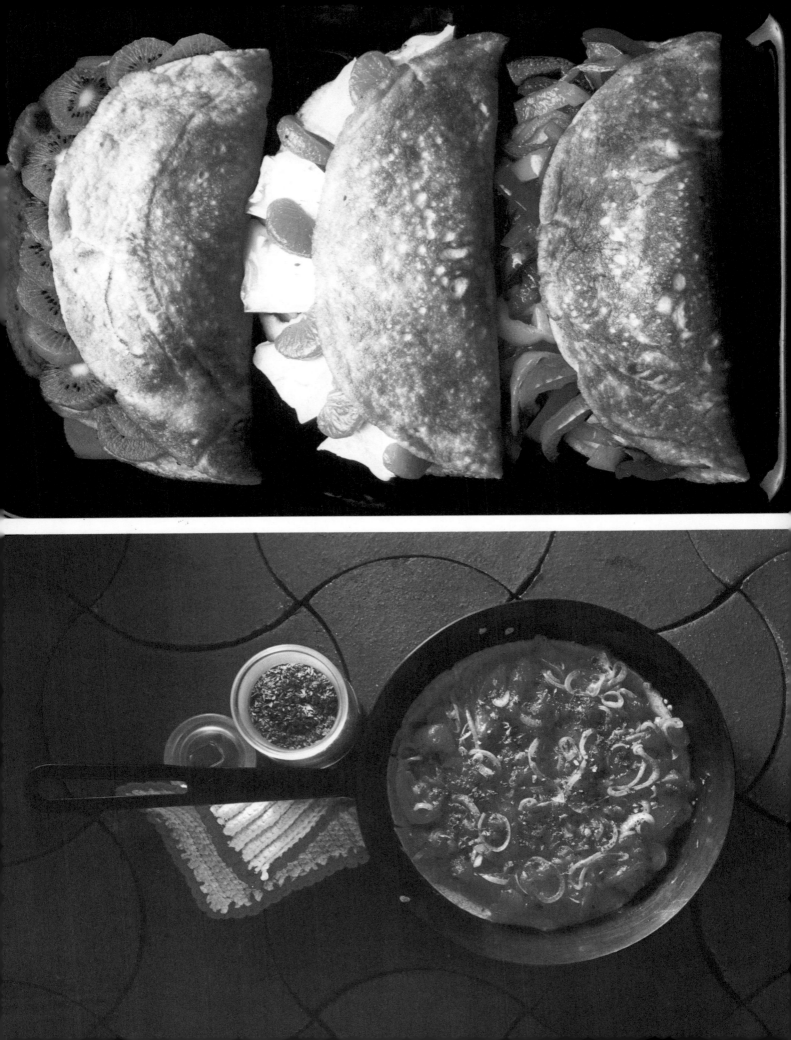

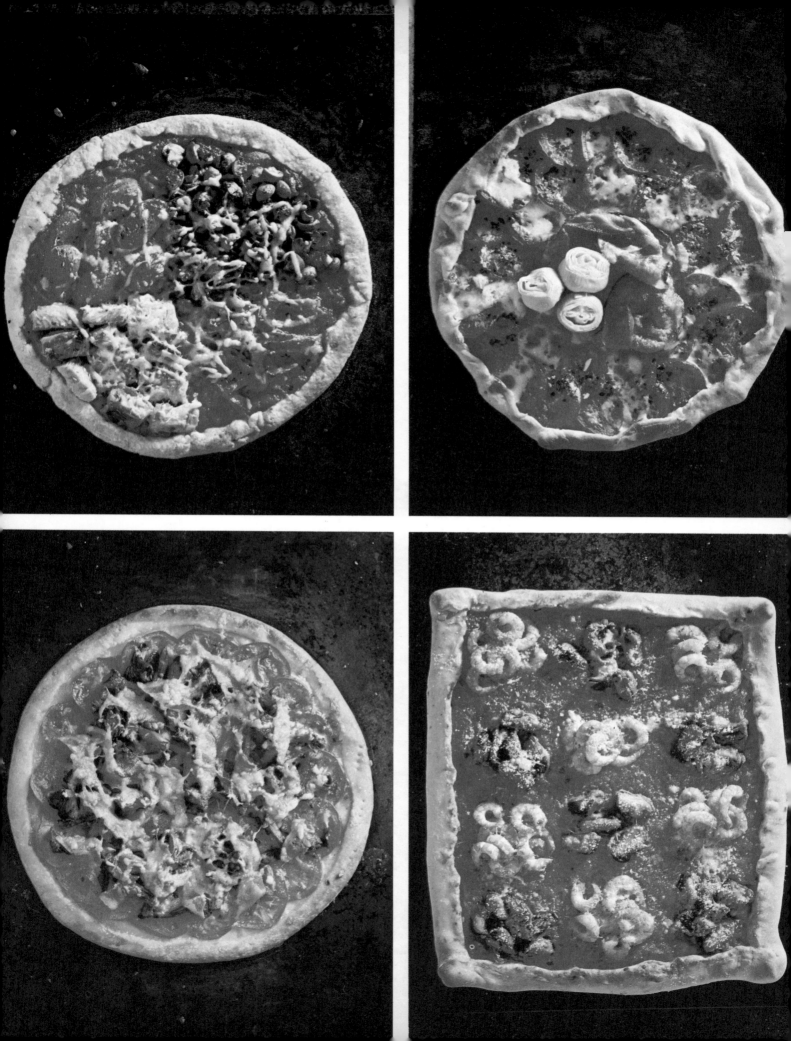

PIZZAS

The word 'pizza' translates simply as 'pie'—yet what an excitingly different meal it makes, and what a host of varieties there are from which to choose! Probably the best known is the Neapolitan, using tomatoes, anchovies and Mozzarella cheese—but here we have selected lots more for you to try. Some are well known and popular ones, others less familiar; but all use the same basic pizza dough base, presented in different ways.

As an extra bonus there are also two recipes using slices of bread in place of the dough. These make delicious snacks for the days when you have less time for preparation, yet still retain a flavour of the Mediterranean to tempt the appetite.

Pizza Napoletana

Preparation and cooking time:
40 minutes
SERVES 4-6

8 oz. pizza dough (see page 62)
6-8 oz. tomatoes, skinned and chopped or ½ pint [1¼ cups] tomato sauce
12 anchovy fillets
about 12 black olives, stoned
¼ teaspoon basil
4-6 slices Mozzarella cheese
1 tablespoon olive oil
freshly ground black pepper

Make up the pizza dough (see page 62). Shape the dough into a round on a floured baking sheet and cover with

---

opposite: from top left: Pizza Quattro Stagioni, Pizza Fiesole, Pizza Capricciosa, Pizza Marina

the chopped tomatoes or tomato sauce. Make a lattice with the anchovy fillets, decorate the pizza with the olives, sprinkle it with basil and pepper and cover it with slices of cheese. Leave the pizza to stand for about 10 minutes.
Heat oven at 400°F (Gas Mark 6, 200°C). Sprinkle the pizza with the olive oil and bake near the top of the oven for 25-30 minutes.

Pizza Fiesole

Preparation and cooking time:
40 minutes
SERVES 4-6

8 oz. pizza dough (see page 62)
6 tomatoes, chopped
6 slices of ham
salt and freshly ground black pepper
2 oz. [½ cup] grated cheese
¼ teaspoon each of oregano and basil
1 tablespoon olive oil
tinned artichoke hearts for garnish

Make up the pizza dough (see page 62). Shape the dough into a round on a floured baking tray, and cover with the chopped tomatoes.
Arrange the slices of ham on top of the tomato. Sprinkle with salt, pepper, and a few pinches of oregano and basil. Top with a generous quantity of grated cheese. Leave to rest in a warm place for 10-15 minutes.
Heat oven to 400°F (Gas Mark 6, 200°C). Moisten the pizza with the olive oil and bake for 25-30 minutes.
Serve on a wooden board, hot or cold, with a tossed mixed salad. Garnish with the tinned, drained and warmed artichoke hearts.

Pizza Quattro Stagioni

Preparation and cooking time:
about 40 minutes
SERVES 4-6

8 oz. of pizza dough (see page 62)
6 tomatoes, skinned and sliced
8 mushrooms, sliced and sautéed in a little butter
8 oz. canned tuna fish in oil
6 thin slices of ham
2 oz. [½ cup] grated cheese
¼ teaspoon basil or oregano
1 tablespoon oil from the tuna fish

Make up the pizza dough (see page 62). Shape the dough into a round on a floured baking tray, and cover with the skinned and sliced tomatoes, the sliced and sautéed mushrooms, flakes of tuna fish, and the thin slices of ham. Sprinkle grated cheese and a little basil or oregano over the top. Leave the pizza to rest for about 10 minutes.
Heat oven to 400°F (Gas Mark 6, 200°C). Moisten the top of the pizza with a little of the oil from the tuna fish and bake at the top of the oven for 25-30 minutes.
To serve transfer the pizza to a wooden board, and serve a tossed green salad separately.

Pizza Margherita

Preparation and cooking time:
about 40 minutes
SERVES 4-6

8 oz. pizza dough (see page 62)
4-6 tomatoes, thinly sliced
8 slices Bel Paese or Mozzarella cheese
salt and pepper
¼ teaspoon oregano
1 tablespoon olive oil

Make up the pizza dough (see page 62). Shape the dough into a round on a floured baking tray, and cover with the sliced tomatoes and cheese. Sprinkle with salt and pepper and oregano. Leave the pizza to rest for about 10 minutes.
Heat oven to 400°F (Gas Mark 6,

200°C). Moisten the pizza with the olive oil and bake at the top of the oven for 25-30 minutes.

Pizza Siciliana

Preparation and cooking time:
about 40 minutes
SERVES 4-6

8 oz. pizza dough (see page 62)
about 5 fl. oz. thick tomato sauce
3 cooked sausages, halved
   lengthwise
12 black olives, sliced
2 oz. [¼ cup] cheese, grated
¼ teaspoon basil
salt and pepper
1 tablespoon olive oil

Make up the pizza dough (see page 62). Shape the dough onto a floured baking sheet. Cover the dough with the tomato sauce, slices of sausage, sliced olives, grated cheese, and sprinkle with basil and salt and pepper. Leave the pizza to stand for about 10 minutes. *Heat* oven to 400°F (Gas Mark 6, 200°C). Moisten the pizza with the olive oil and bake at the top of the oven for 25-30 minutes.

Pizza Calzone

Preparation and cooking time:
about 40 minutes
SERVES 4-6

8 oz. pizza dough (see page 62)
8 slices of ham
8 slices of Mozzarella cheese
1 tablespoon olive oil
salt and pepper

Make up the pizza dough (see page 62). Cut the dough into rounds approximately the size of a small plate. Lay a slice of ham and a slice of Mozzarella cheese on each round. Sprinkle with olive oil, salt, and pepper. Fold over the dough into a half moon shape. Press down the edges firmly. Leave the pizzas to stand for about 10 minutes. *Heat* oven to 400°F (Gas Mark 6,

200°C). Bake at the top of the oven for about 20 minutes, until the dough is puffed up and brown.

Pizza Capricciosa

Preparation and cooking time:
40 minutes
SERVES 4-6

8 oz. pizza dough (see page 62)
4 tomatoes, sliced
6 slices of ham or cooked bacon
8 mushrooms, sliced and sautéed
   in a little butter
6-8 oz. Bel Paese cheese, sliced
¼ teaspoon oregano
1 tablespoon olive oil

Make up the pizza dough (see page 62). *Shape* the dough into a round on a floured baking tray, cover with sliced tomatoes, slices of ham or bacon and the sautéed mushrooms. Cover the topping with the cheese, and sprinkle with a little oregano. Leave the pizza to rest for about 10 minutes. *Heat* oven to 400°F (Gas Mark 6, 200°C). Moisten the top of the pizza with a little olive oil and bake at the top of the oven for 25-30 minutes.

Pizza Marina

Preparation and cooking time:
about 40 minutes
SERVES 4-6

8 oz. pizza dough (see page 62)
5 fl. oz. thick tomato sauce
¼ lb. [1 cup] shrimps, cooked and
   peeled
12 mussels or clams, shelled
2 oz. [½ cup] grated cheese
¼ teaspoon oregano
salt and pepper
1 tablespoon olive oil

Make up the pizza dough (see page 62). Shape the dough into a square or oblong, on a floured baking tray, and cover with tomato sauce, shrimps, mussels or clams, cheese and a sprinkling of oregano, and salt and pepper. Leave the pizza to stand for about 10 minutes.

Heat oven to 400°F (Gas Mark 6, 200°C). Moisten the pizza with a little olive oil and bake near the top of the oven for 25-30 minutes.
Serve the pizza cut into squares.

Pizza Sandwich

Preparation and cooking time:
10 minutes
SERVES 1

1 slice of white bread
1 large tomato, sliced
salt, pepper and oregano
4-6 sardines
2-3 black olives, stoned
1 slice of Mozzarella cheese

Butter the slice of bread and cover with the sliced tomato, sprinkle with salt, pepper and a little oregano. Place the sardines on top, garnish with the stoned olives, and lay the slice of cheese over the olives. Place under the grill [broiler] and cook until the cheese is melted and slightly browned. *Serve* at once.

French Pizza Sandwich

Preparation and cooking time:
15 minutes
SERVES 1

1 section of French bread cut in
   half lengthwise
4-6 slices of ham
a few mushrooms
1 large tomato, sliced
2 oz. [½ cup] grated cheese

Butter the bread and cover with the slices of ham. Slice the mushrooms and sauté them in a little butter. Top the ham with the slices of tomato and the sautéed mushrooms. Sprinkle liberally with the grated cheese. Place under the grill [broiler] and cook until the cheese has melted and started to turn brown.
Serve at once.

---

opposite: Pizza Margherita, Pizza Calzone

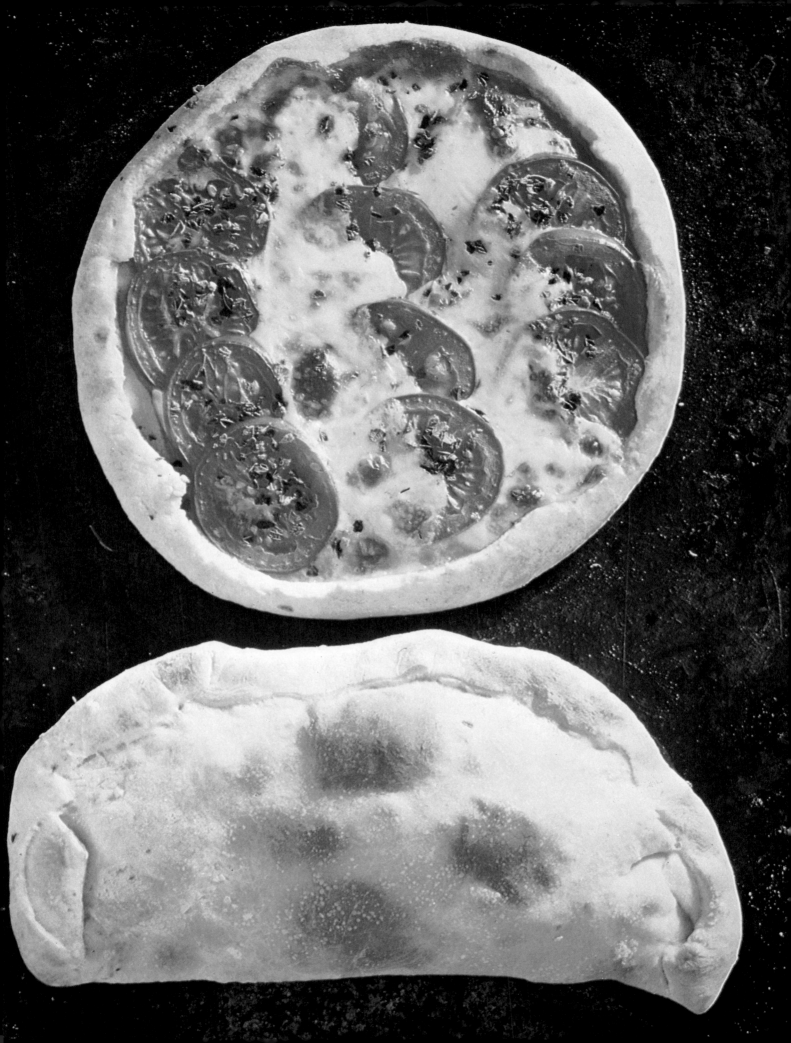

FONDUES

Today many people have the equipment necessary for cooking fondues—and there is no doubt that this can make an excellent and entertaining meal. A beef fondue tends to be expensive—so here we give recipes for less costly, but equally tasty, fondues. The Cheese Fondue can make a meal in itself when served with salads—and it is a substantial dish, so follow it with a fresh fruit salad if you want a dessert, for a crisp and light conclusion to the meal. Poor Man's Fondue needs lots of accompanying sauces—use some of the chutneys and sauces in the basic recipes section as well as those listed. Or for a change try the Mock Fondue.

below: Cheese Fondue

Poor Man's Fondue

☆　　①　　⬤

Preparation time:
30 minutes

For each person allow about eight chunks of bread; white bread is best. Place these on a large platter and let your guests help themselves.

Heat vegetable oil in the fondue pan until it is sufficiently hot. Then the pan may be placed on the spirit stove and kept hot at the table.
A cube of bread is speared on a fondue fork and put in the hot fat until it is crisp. It is then dipped into one of the sauces.

Serve the following sauces in small bowls
§ *Piquant tomato sauce* (see Cheese Fondue)

§ *Devilled ham sauce:*
5 fl. oz. mayonnaise
½ teaspoon curry powder
1 teaspoon made mustard
1 tablespoon mango chutney
4 oz. [½ cup] finely chopped ham
salt and pepper

Mix the mayonnaise with the curry powder and mustard, then add the mango chutney and ham and season to taste.

§ *Garlic-cheese sauce.*
Blend together 4 oz of cottage cheese and 4 oz of cream cheese, 1 tablespoon of very finely chopped onion, and 1 clove of garlic crushed together with ½ teaspoon of salt. Season the sauce with a little paprika.

§ *Quick celery sauce.*
Mix the contents of a 1½ pint [3¾ cup] packet of celery soup with ½ pint [1¼ cups] of sour cream. Season with salt and pepper and leave as long as possible before serving to allow the flavours time to blend.

§ *Pâté and tomato sauce.*
Cream 8 oz. of canned liver pâté with enough mayonnaise and tomato ketchup to make a smooth sauce. Stir in 1 teaspoon of made mustard and season with salt and pepper.

Small bowls of black olives, gherkins, radishes and cubed cucumber may also be served as accompaniments.

The Poor Man's Fondue is ideal as a vegetarian dish. Individual cheese soufflés could be served to start the meal, and a fruit sorbet or a large bowl of fresh fruit salad, a cheese board and a large bowl of mixed nuts would be suitable to complete it. Alternatively the meal could begin with a selection of salami and other cold meats, or a mixed fish hors d'oeuvres of tuna, crab, sardine, prawn or shrimp and anchovy. Or serve one fish dish such as mussels with a vinaigrette dressing of 8 tablespoons of olive oil, 4 tablespoons of red wine vinegar, a little garlic salt, freshly ground black pepper, and a little chopped mixed herbs.

Cheese Fondue

☆ ☆　①①　◖

Preparation time:
15 minutes
S E R V E S 4

1 clove of garlic, crushed
8 fl. oz. [1 cup] dry white wine
½ lb. Emmenthal [Swiss] cheese
½ lb. Gruyère cheese
1 glass Kirsch
1½ teaspoons cornflour [cornstarch]
pepper and a little nutmeg
1 French loaf, cut into small cubes

Rub a fireproof, ceramic or earthenware casserole with the clove of garlic. Pour in the white wine, and add the coarsely grated cheeses. Stir continuously over a medium heat until the cheese is melted and is creamy in consistency.
Add the Kirsch, mixed with the cornflour, pepper and nutmeg.
Keep hot on a spirit stove. The guests spear a cube of bread on their fondue forks and dip into the cheese mixture.
Serve with a selection of sauces or salads in individual dishes.

Piquant tomato sauce
1 tablespoon mayonnaise
5 fl. oz. bottled tomato ketchup or sauce
½ an onion, grated
salt
2 dashes Tabasco sauce

Mix all the ingredients together, seasoning carefully with a little Tabasco sauce.

Accompanying Salads:
§ Cooked corn mixed with sliced cooked red pepper and tossed in a vinaigrette dressing.
§ Tossed green salad of lettuce, watercress, chicory [endive], celery, sliced green pepper and cucumber.
§ Cooked green peas, carefully mixed with quarters of skinned tomatoes.

Mock Fondue

☆　　①　　◑

Preparation and cooking time:
10 minutes
S E R V E S 1-2

2 tablespoons butter
2 tablespoons flour
5 fl. oz. milk
salt and a pinch of nutmeg
pinch of cayenne pepper
2 oz. [½ cup] grated Gruyère or Chedder cheese
2 slices of hot buttered toast
a little made mustard

Melt the butter in a heavy based saucepan. Remove it from the heat and stir in the flour. Gradually blend the milk into the flour and butter mixture then return to the heat and bring to the boil, stirring all the time until thickened. Allow the sauce to simmer for a few minutes, and gradually beat the cheese into it. Season with salt, nutmeg, and a pinch of cayenne pepper.
Spread a little mustard on each piece of toast and arrange the toast in a shallow dish. Pour the sauce over it and serve immediately.

Variations:
§ Scatter a few sliced gherkins over the hot buttered toast before pouring over the sauce.
§ Arrange a layer of 4 skinned, sliced and sautéed tomatoes with a pinch of dried basil on top of the hot buttered toast just before pouring over the sauce.
§ Spread the hot buttered toast with a little anchovy paste before pouring over the cheese sauce.

To make a more substantial dish serve the mock fondue with rolls of thinly sliced cooked ham—about two rolls per person—and serve a mixed green salad separately.

FLAMBÉED FOOD

Serving flambéed food requires a little care, and sometimes some special equipment. If you wish to flame the dish at the table you will need a special flambé pan, and a table burner. The most usual spirits to achieve the flaming are brandy or rum, as used in these recipes, but for a sweet dessert you could use an appropriate liqueur instead.

There is no doubt that such a dish will provide an impressive climax to any meal—but do remember that the courses which precede or follow a flambé should be comparatively simple ones, and that the accompaniments must be understated: a green salad; some plainly boiled rice.

Pork Rolls Flambé

☆ ☆ ☆ ① ① ① ⏲

Preparation and cooking time:
30 minutes
SERVES 4

4 slices of bacon
4 sprigs of parsley
4 thin slices of lean pork
salt and pepper
1 tablespoon oil
3 tablespoons butter
1 small can of mandarin oranges
10 stuffed olives
5 oz. black grapes
1 tablespoon mustard
3 tablespoons white wine
a few dashes Worcestershire sauce
3 tablespoons rum

Put a slice of bacon and a sprig of parsley on each of the pieces of pork, season with salt and pepper and roll up. Secure the rolls with a wooden skewer or with thread. Heat the butter and oil in a frying pan and brown the pork rolls well on all sides or grill [broil]. Add the liquid from the tin of mandarin oranges, put on the pan lid and cook gently for 15 minutes.
Meanwhile halve the olives and halve

opposite: Pork Rolls Flambé

and pip the grapes. Add the olives, mandarin oranges, and grapes, with the mustard, wine and Worcestershire sauce to the pan. Mix together well and cook for another few minutes. Warm the rum in a small saucepan or soup ladle, set light to it and pour it flaming over the pork, rotating the pan. Serve at once.
The flaming of the food may be carried out at the table, in which case a flambé pan and a small table cooker must be used to cook the pork.

Chicken Kebabs Flambé

☆ ☆ ☆ ① ① ① ⏲

Preparation and cooking time:
30 minutes, excluding marinating time
SERVES 4

1 large roasting chicken
4 tablespoons white wine
2 tablespoons oil
5 tablespoons soy sauce
16 button mushrooms
1 small can pineapple rings
1 large orange
8 cherries
salt and paprika
4 tablespoons butter
4 tablespoons brandy

Remove the skin and bones from the chicken, and cut the meat into cubes. Mix together the white wine, oil and soy sauce. Marinade the chicken meat in this mixture for about 15-20 minutes.
Clean and wash the mushrooms. Drain the pineapple and cut it into cubes. Peel the orange and halve the segments. Stone the cherries if necessary. Thread all these ingredients including the drained chicken cubes, alternately on to eight skewers, and sprinkle them with salt and paprika.
Heat the butter in a large frying pan and fry the kebabs until they are browned on all sides and the chicken is cooked. Pour the brandy into the pan and light, rotating the pan with the chicken in it so that the brandy is

evenly distributed. Serve still burning.
Serve with rice and a green salad.

Variations:
Different ingredients may be used instead of those used in the recipe, or could be added to them. Try rolls of thin bacon, or stoned prunes to replace the pineapple or orange.

Prawn Flambé

☆ ☆ ☆ ① ① ① ◗

Preparation and cooking time:
10 minutes
SERVES 4 (as a first course)

1 small onion
1½ oz. [3 tablespoons] butter
¼ lb. button mushrooms
8 oz. cooked and shelled prawns or shrimps
salt and freshly ground black pepper
lemon juice and nutmeg
3 tablespoons brandy
5 fl. oz. double [heavy] cream
chopped parsley
plain boiled rice

Peel and finely chop the onion. Melt the butter in a frying pan, and soften the onion in it. Clean the mushrooms and halve or quarter depending on their size. Add the prawns or shrimps and mushrooms to the pan and sauté them gently for a few minutes. Season this mixture well with the salt, pepper, lemon juice and nutmeg.
Warm the brandy in a soup ladle or large spoon, ignite it and pour it flaming over the prawn mixture, rotate the pan to spread the flames. When the flames have gone out, leave the pan a few minutes over a very gentle heat, then add the cream, turn up the heat and boil it until it starts to thicken, ensuring that all the contents of the pan are kept moving and that the cream is well mixed in.
Serve the prawns or shrimps on top of the plain boiled rice and decorate with chopped parsley.

Variation:
To serve as a main dish, add a few peeled, and quartered tomatoes with the seeds removed, and use about 12 ounces of prawns or shrimps. Serve with plain boiled rice and a green salad of lettuce, watercress and avocado slices.

ORIENTAL FOOD

An Oriental dish is typically one in which the cooking time is kept to a minimum, and so the flavour of each ingredient remains clearly distinct from the others and all are crisp and fresh. This requires careful preparation of the food—but once everything is ready to cook, you are only minutes away from a truly different meal.

Only the Chinese Soup requires a special utensil; here a fondue pan would be perfectly adequate. Unless you have a 'wok' or Chinese cooking pan use a large saucepan or frying pan for the other dishes. Serve the Chinese dishes with China tea, and the Japanese dish with sake (rice wine).

left: Chinese Sweet and Sour Pork
below: Chinese Soup

Chinese Soup

☆ ☆   ① ① ① ⏰

Preparation and cooking time:
40 minutes
S E R V E S 4

1 medium-sized roasting chicken
1 bouquet garni
1 medium-sized onion
1 bay leaf
2 pints [5 cups] water
4 oz. [1 cup] mushrooms, sliced
1 red pepper, shredded
4 oz. [½ cup] bamboo shoots
4 oz. [½ cup] celery or cabbage,
  shredded
4 oz. [½ cup] water chestnut, sliced
8 oz. [1 cup] cooked rice
½ lb. lobster meat or large prawns
  or shrimps

Remove the skin and flesh from the chicken. Place the bones in a large pan, with the bouquet garni, onion, bay leaf and water, and boil for 30 minutes to make stock.
Meanwhile cut the chicken flesh into small chunks and arrange the rest of the ingredients attractively in bowls (as shown in the photograph).
Strain the stock into a large pan and place it on a spirit heater in the centre of the dining table—make sure it is brought back to the boil and kept simmering. Put some of the vegetables and lobster (or prawns or shrimps) with all of the chicken pieces into the stock, and leave them to simmer.
Let each person serve himself with the help of long fondue forks or chop sticks, cooking the food they choose for a few minutes in the stock, like a fondue. Serve with rice, china tea and different sauces. We suggest the Oriental Sauce and the Thick Tomato Sauce.

Chinese Sweet and Sour Pork

☆   ① ①   ◑

Preparation and cooking time:
20 minutes
S E R V E S 4

1 lb. lean raw pork
2 medium-sized carrots
2 small green peppers

2 tablespoons butter or
  2 tablespoons oil
4 oz. [1 cup] green peas
For the sauce:
2 tablespoons soy sauce
5 fl. oz. stock or water
1 tablespoon cornflour [cornstarch]
1 tablespoon brown sugar
1 tablespoon vinegar
salt

Cut the pork into thin slices. Slice the prepared carrots and peppers thinly. Heat the oil or butter in a shallow pan, and add the pork slices. Sauté them quickly for a few minutes. Add the vegetables and sauté for a further three minutes.
Mix the ingredients for the sauce together and pour them over the pork and vegetable mixture. Stir the mixture steadily until it comes to the boil. Cover the pan and simmer for a further ten minutes stirring frequently. Season with a little more vinegar, salt and sugar if necessary. The pork should be cooked and the vegetables should still be crisp.
Serve with plain boiled rice.

Chinese Steak and Cauliflower

☆   ① ① ① ⏰

Preparation and cooking time:
30 minutes
S E R V E S 4

1 cauliflower
1 lb. rump steak
2 medium-sized onions
2 tablespoons oil
2 cloves of garlic
2 tablespoons soy sauce
8 fl. oz. [1 cup] water
¼ teaspoon freshly ground pepper
1 level teaspoon cornflour
  [cornstarch] (**optional**)

Trim the cauliflower, and cut it into small 'bite-sized' florets. Trim the fat off the steak and, with a sharp knife, cut it into thin slices approximately $\frac{1}{10}$th-inch thick and 2-inches long.
Heat half the oil in a large frying pan or 'wok' and add the peeled garlic. Keep the cloves moving all the time, and remove them as soon as they start to go brown so that the oil is left with the flavour. Peel the onions and cut them in wedges. Fry these in the oil until they are just starting

to colour, then remove them from the pan.
Reheat the remaining oil in pan until it is smoking hot, and add the steak, browning it quickly and stirring continuously. Return the onions to the pan and add the cauliflower florets, soy sauce, water and pepper. Bring to the boil, then reduce the heat, stir, and cover. Simmer for 4 minutes or a little longer if preferred. Blend the cornflour with some liquid from the pan, pour this over the meat, stir and bring to the boil again. Reduce the heat and simmer gently for 2-3 minutes, stirring all the time.
Serve with plain boiled or fried rice.

Japanese Chicken and Vegetables

☆ ☆   ① ①   ⏰

Preparation and cooking time:
25 minutes
S E R V E S 4

6 spring onions [scallions]
1 tablespoon oil
6 oz. [1 cup] long-grain rice
1 pint [2½ cups] water
2 carrots, grated
6 mushrooms, sliced
1½ teaspoons sugar
1 teaspoon salt
¼ teaspoon pepper
6 mange-tout [snow peas]
2 tablespoons soy sauce
8 oz. [1 cup] shredded, cooked
  chicken meat
dash of monosodium glutamate
  (optional)

Trim the onions, chop them finely and remove the ends from the mange-tout. Heat the oil in a large saucepan and fry the onions until they are tender but not browned.
Add the rice and cook until all the oil is absorbed. Add the water, carrots, mushrooms, sugar, salt, pepper and soy sauce and bring to the boil, stirring. Reduce the heat to a minimum, cover the pan and cook gently for about 20 minutes or until the rice is cooked.
Meanwhile cook the mange-tout in boiling salted water for 2-3 minutes or until they are tender. Drain and sprinkle with monosodium glutamate.
When the rice is cooked stir in the chicken, adjust the seasoning and serve decorated with the mange-tout.

97

SEAFOOD

These recipes take full advantage of the wealth of flavour available in most seafoods. These often tend to be regarded as luxury foods, but are often no more expensive than good quality meat—and usually require less preparation and a shorter cooking time.

Many of the dishes here would make excellent first courses, while most could well be served as a satisfying main course, too. Always ensure when fish is served that the flavours of the other courses do not 'kill' that of the fish—so keep the entire meal a contrast of subtle rather than flamboyant flavours.

left: Crêpes with Creamed Shellfish
below: Scampi in White Wine Sauce

Scampi in White Wine Sauce

✩ ✩   ① ① ①

Preparation and cooking time:
20 minutes
S E R V E S 4

2 tablespoons butter
4 tablespoons flour
5 fl. oz. milk
5 fl. oz. single [light] cream
4 fl. oz. white wine
salt
¼ teaspoon French mustard
small pinch of tarragon
pinch of cayenne pepper
1 lb. cooked scampi or shrimps

Melt the butter, remove the pan from the heat and blend in the flour. Gradually stir in the milk and cream and add the white wine. Season with the salt, mustard, tarragon and cayenne pepper. Bring the sauce to the boil, stirring all the time, and simmer until thickened and smooth. Just before serving, add the scampi and gently heat through. Take care not to overcook the scampi as this spoils their flavour and appearance.
Serve with plain boiled rice and a tomato and watercress salad.

Crêpes with Creamed Shellfish

✩ ✩   ① ①   ●

Preparation and cooking time:
30 minutes
S E R V E S 4

For the crêpe batter:
4 oz. [1 cup] flour
½ teaspoon salt
1 egg
1 egg yolk
½ pint [1¼ cups] milk
1 tablespoon melted butter
For the filling:
2 tablespoons butter
4 tablespoons flour
12 fl. oz. [1½ cups] single [light]
   cream and milk mixed in equal
   quantities
salt and pepper
8 oz. canned crabmeat
a little grated cheese

Sift the flour and salt into a bowl. Make a well in the centre of it and drop in the whole egg and extra yolk. Gradually mix in the milk. When half the liquid has been added stir in the melted butter. Add the rest of the liquid and beat well. Cover the batter and leave it to stand while preparing the filling.
Melt the butter, remove the pan from the heat and blend in the flour and the milk and cream mixture. Bring to the boil stirring well, season, and cook for a few minutes. Stir in the crabmeat.
Make the crêpes, ensuring that they are thin, and stacking them on top of each other on a wire rack as they are being cooked.
Place a large spoonful of crab mixture on each crêpe, roll up and place in a warm buttered heatproof dish. Sprinkle with a little grated cheese, and brown under the grill [broiler] for 5 minutes.

Shrimp Salad

✩   ① ①   ◑

Preparation and cooking time:
20 minutes
S E R V E S 4 as a first course

2 tablespoons lemon juice
3 tablespoons olive oil
a dash of Worcestershire or
   Tabasco sauce
salt and freshly ground black
   pepper
½ lb. [2 cups] shrimps or prawns,
   cooked and shelled
4 stalks raw celery
1 green pepper
1 eating apple
8 shelled walnut halves
3 tablespoons mayonnaise
2 tablespoons single [light] cream
lettuce
finely chopped parsley

Mix together the lemon juice, oil and dash of Worcestershire or Tabasco sauce. Add a little salt and pepper and pour over the shrimps and leave them to marinate for a little while. Chop the celery and the green pepper, from which the seeds have been removed. Chop the apple and sprinkle it with a little lemon juice to prevent discolouration.
Chop the walnuts and mix them with the apple, celery, green pepper, and shrimps drained from their marinade.

Season to taste. Fold the cream into the mayonnaise. Shred the lettuce and arrange it on a serving dish. Fold the mayonnaise and cream into the shrimp mixture. Spoon in a heap on to the bed of lettuce and sprinkle with a little chopped parsley.

Potted Shellfish

✩   ① ① ① ●

Preparation and cooking time:
15 minutes
S E R V E S 4

¾ lb. freshly boiled shellfish meat e.g.
   lobster, crab, scampi, prawns or
   shrimps
4 tablespoons butter
½ teaspoon freshly ground pepper
good pinch of cayenne pepper
¼ teaspoon ground mace
¼ teaspoon salt

Mash any large pieces of shellfish meat in a mortar (shrimps may be left whole). Put the shellfish meat into a large saucepan with about half the butter and all the seasonings. Toss this in melted butter until heated through but not fried. Put into small pots.
Melt the remaining butter and pour over the pots of shellfish meat. Leave in a cool place until the butter sets.
Cover each pot with circles of waxed paper and cover with foil. Store in a cool place or in the refrigerator for 4-6 days.
Serve with hot buttered toast or with brown bread and butter, as a first course.

Paella

✩ ✩   ① ① ① ●

Preparation and cooking time:
30 minutes
S E R V E S 4-6

1 onion
1 clove of garlic
5 tablespoons oil
12 oz. [2 cups] long-grain rice
1 pt. [2½ cups] chicken stock, heated
½ boiled or fried chicken
1 tinned sweet red pimiento
1 can mussels
¼ teaspoon saffron
½ lb. shelled shrimps or prawns

8 oz. green peas
1 small jar stuffed olives
salt and pepper

Chop the onion and finely chop the garlic, and fry them in the hot oil until they are transparent. Add the rice and cook for 3-5 minutes. Pour in the hot chicken stock cover with a lid and cook the rice until it is almost tender for about 7-10 minutes, adding a little more stock if necessary.
Meanwhile cut the chicken flesh into pieces and slice the sweet red pepper. When the rice is almost cooked stir in the chicken meat, the drained mussels, sliced pepper, saffron, shelled shrimps or prawns and peas and stuffed olives. Season to taste.
Return the pan to the heat and continue to heat the rest of the ingredients through. The paella should be fairly dry.

Variation:
Fish such as scallops and clams may be added with peeled and chopped tomatoes.

Note: If using saffron filaments rather than the powdered variety, subtract 5 fluid ounces from the stock allowance, place the saffron in it, bring to the boil, remove from the heat and allow to soak. Add it, strained, at the appropriate moment.

Mussels in White Wine

☆ ☆ ☆ ① ① ◑

Preparation and cooking time:
25 minutes
SERVES 4 as a first course

1 quart mussels
1 large onion, chopped
1 stalk celery, chopped
parsley stalks and a sprig of thyme
1 bay leaf and 3 peppercorns
4 fl. oz. dry white wine
3 tablespoons butter
4 tablespoons flour
1 pt. [2½ cups] water or vegetable stock
salt and freshly ground black pepper
garlic powder
a little chopped parsley

Wash the mussels in plenty of cold water and scrub them very well. Remove the 'beard' or sea-weed like bits protruding from the shell, and

discard mussels that are open or which do not close tightly when sharply tapped: these are dead. Wash them in several changes of water until the water is free from grit. Place the mussels in a large pan with half of the chopped onion, and celery, peppercorns, parsley stalks, sprig of thyme and a bay leaf. Pour in the wine, cover the pan tightly, and bring to the boil quickly, shaking frequently. Cook for about 6-8 minutes or until the shells have opened. Discard any shells which do not open.
Leave the mussels to one side in a warm dish and strain the cooking liquid through a fine strainer or muslin. Melt the butter and gently sauté the rest of the chopped onion. Remove from the heat, stir in the flour, and gradually blend in the water or vegetable stock. Return to the heat and stir continuously until boiling, then season with salt, freshly ground black pepper and a little garlic powder. Pour the sauce over the mussels, sprinkle with parsley and serve immediately.
Serve in deep plates with plenty of crusty bread.

Baked Scallops au Gratin

☆ ☆ ① ① ◑

Preparation and cooking time:
25 minutes
SERVES 4

8 scallops
5 fl. oz. white wine (or white wine and fish stock)
1 small onion
salt and pepper
1 small bay leaf
⅛ teaspoon ground mace
For the sauce:
2 tablespoons butter
1 oz. [4 tablespoons] flour
5 fl. oz. milk
2 tablespoons single [light] cream
2 oz. [8 tablespoons] Cheddar cheese, grated
To garnish:
slices of lemon
sprigs of parsley

Heat oven to 350°F (Gas Mark 4, 180°C).
Remove scallops from their shells

and discard the beards. Slice the white part and put this together with the red part into a heatproof dish. Add the wine.
Peel the onion and cut into quarters (so that the pieces are big enough to remove later). Add the onion, salt, pepper, bay leaf and mace. Cover with aluminium foil or greaseproof [waxed] paper and bake until tender (about 10 minutes).
Meanwhile prepare the sauce using the butter, flour and milk, then add the liquor from the scallops' cooking liquid. Beat in the cream and half the grated cheese and adjust the seasoning to taste. Pour a little sauce into 4 scallop shells, place the pieces of cooked scallops on top and cover with the remaining sauce. Sprinkle with the rest of the grated cheese and brown under the grill [broiler].
Garnish with lemon and parsley and serve.

Crayfish Soup

☆ ① ◑

Preparation and cooking time:
20 minutes
SERVES 4-6

1 small onion
3 tablespoons butter
4 tablespoons flour
1¼ pts. [3 cups] chicken stock
2½ fl. oz. dry white wine
1 can crayfish tails or ¼ lb. cooked prawns or shrimps
6 oz. cooked peas
salt and freshly ground black pepper
a few spoonfuls of single [light] cream

Peel and finely chop the onion. Gently fry it in the melted butter without letting it brown. Add the flour to the pan and stir in the butter. Pour in the stock and bring to the boil, stirring all the time. Cook for a few minutes. Pour in the wine and add the fish and peas—heat through very gently. Season to taste and stir in a few spoonfuls of cream. If the sauce is too thick add a little more stock before the cream.
Serve with warmed French bread.

opposite: back: mussels for Mussels in White Wine, Crayfish Soup front: Paella

GRILLED MEATS

If you are working against time to prepare a complete meal, a grill makes an excellent choice for the main dish. Start with a canned or packet soup, adding extra ingredients for flavour and texture (the Senegalese Soup would be a good idea). Add savoury rice or creamy mashed potatoes with a salad, or make one of the quick vegetable dishes. Finish with fresh fruit and cheese with biscuits (crackers) to satisfy the largest appetites.

below: Grilled [Broiled] Ham Steak

Grilled (broiled) Ham Steak

☆ ① ① ●

Preparation and cooking time:
30 minutes
SERVES 2

1 slice of fresh gammon or ham
   (about 1 lb.)
freshly ground black pepper
a pinch of oregano
6 tomatoes
2 tablespoons melted butter
a squeeze of lemon juice
pinch of basil

Cut the rind off the gammon or ham, and snip the fat at intervals, to avoid the meat curling up during cooking. Place the meat on the grill [broiler] pan and sprinkle with pepper and oregano. It is best not to add salt at this stage as ham varies greatly in its salt content.
Grill [broil] for 10 to 15 minutes, depending on the thickness. Turn the meat, season again and grill for a further 10 to 15 minutes on the other side.
Slit the tomatoes in a cross on the top and pour in the butter, and lemon juice. Sprinkle with salt, pepper and basil and place under the grill [broiler] for the last five minutes.

Variations:
§ Omit the tomatoes and grill [broil] four peach halves from a tin, for about 5 minutes.
§ Serve with fried apple rings and omit the tomatoes.
§ Serve with a sauce of 3 tablespoons of brown sugar, melted in 5 fluid ounces of orange or pineapple juice, and boiled together for a few minutes.

Lamb Kebab

Preparation and cooking time:
30 minutes
SERVES 4

1 medium-sized onion
1 small green pepper
1 small red pepper
2 tablespoons butter
3 teaspoons curry powder
1 teaspoon garam masala

3 tablespoons flour
½-¾ pint [1¼-1⅞ cups] stock (or water
   and a stock cube)
1 clove of garlic
1½ lb. thick lamb chump chops or
   leg of lamb
4 small onions
bay leaves
oil

Peel and chop the onion. Cut peppers in half, remove white pith and seeds, and chop the flesh.
Melt the butter in a covered frying pan (use aluminium foil if a lid is not available) and sauté the onions and peppers lightly for 2-3 minutes. Add most of the curry powder, flour and garam masala, and cook for about 1 minute. Remove from the heat and slowly add the stock, stirring continuously.
Turn the grill [broiler] on to full heat.
Peel and crush the garlic, and add it to the onion and pepper mixture. Return to the heat and stir until it has thickened. Reduce, cover and simmer for a few minutes.
Trim any excess fat from the chops and cut the meat into ¾-inch cubes; sprinkle with the remaining curry powder. Peel and cut the 4 small onions into wedges. Thread on to the skewers the meat, onions and bay leaves alternately. Brush liberally with oil and grill [broil] until browned, turning frequently (about 5-8 minutes).
Place the skewers in the sauce and simmer for a few minutes until the lamb is tender. Serve with plain boiled rice.

Grilled Lamb Chops

☆ ① ① ◑

Preparation and cooking time:
20 minutes
SERVES 4

8 loin lamb chops (¾-inch thick)
salt and freshly ground pepper

Preheat grill [broiler] for 5 minutes on a high setting. Wipe and trim off excess fat from chops. With a sharp knife make slanting cuts in the fat at the edge of the chops at one inch intervals—this is so that the chops do not curl.
Sprinkle with salt and pepper.

Put the chops on a rack and grill [broil]. After 5 minutes turn and grill for a further 5 minutes or until cooked. Serve on very hot plates with vegetables and mint sauce or with redcurrant jelly.

Variations:
§ Lamb chops are delicious with slices of bacon. Put the bacon on top of the chops and grill [broil] for about 2 minutes on either side, then remove the bacon and keep hot. Continue to grill the chops for a further 4 minutes on either side.
§ *Stuffed Lamb Chops:* Remove the bones from the chops. Place half a skinned lamb's kidney in place of the bone. Wrap the lamb chop round it, securing with a toothpick. Grill [broil] 6 minutes on either side. Remove the toothpick before serving.

Tournedos Rossini
(with mushroom and Madeira sauce)

☆ ☆ ① ① ① ◑

Preparation and cooking time:
20 minutes
SERVES 4

¼ lb. mushrooms
4 tablespoons butter
1 shallot or small onion
2 tablespoons flour
15 fl. oz. [2 cups] beef stock,
4 fl. oz. Madeira wine
salt and pepper
4 tablespoons butter
freshly ground black pepper
4 tournedos [small trimmed fillet
   steaks]
4 slices pâté [to fit top of steaks]
4 slices white bread

Wash, dry and slice the mushrooms. Melt half the butter in a saucepan, sauté the mushrooms until tender, and remove them from the pan.
Peel and chop the shallot or onion, add it to the remaining butter and sauté until it is tender but not browned. Blend in the flour and cook for about 1 minute. Remove from the heat and add the stock slowly, stirring all the time. Add the wine.
Return to the heat and bring to the boil, stirring until thickened. Simmer for about 5 minutes. Season with salt and pepper to taste.

103

Pre-heat the grill [broiler] to a high setting. Dot the steaks with butter and sprinkle with the freshly ground pepper. Grill [broil] for about 4 minutes on each side (or to taste). Meanwhile melt 4 tablespoons of butter in a frying pan and fry the bread on both sides.
Remove the steaks from the grill and keep hot. Place the slices of pâté in the meat juices and return to the grill to heat through.
To serve place a steak on each croûton with a slice of pâté on top. Pour the meat juices into the sauce, then strain and add the mushroom slices. Re-heat and serve separately.

Mixed Grill

☆ ☆   ① ①   ●

Preparation and cooking time:
30 minutes
SERVES 4

4 lamb chops (cut about 1-inch
    thick)
4 pork sausages
4 slices lamb's liver
4 slices bacon
4 tomatoes
8 mushrooms
2 tablespoons butter
salt and pepper
bunch of watercress

Heat the grill [broiler] on a high setting.
Start the lamb chops and the sausages first, since these will take about 15 minutes to cook. Wipe and trim the chops and place on the grill [broiler] tray with the sausages, remembering to turn the sausages gradually as they brown, and to lower the heat when the chops are browned on both sides. Meanwhile wash and trim the liver, and pat it dry with absorbent paper. Sprinkle each piece with salt and pepper, and add a small knob of butter to each piece.
After about 8 minutes add the liver to the grill [broiler] tray, each slice with a slice of bacon on top. Grill for about 2 minutes [or longer if you like crisp bacon] then turn the bacon and grill the other side as well. Remove the bacon as it is cooked and keep hot on a serving dish. Turn the liver and cook for a further few minutes.
When the chops and sausages are cooked remove these too to keep hot.

Cut the tomatoes in half and place on the grill [broiler] tray with the mushrooms, dotted with butter and sprinkled with salt and pepper. Grill these for about 2-3 minutes, then add to the serving dish.
Garnish the dish with watercress and serve with redcurrant jelly for the chops, and mustard for the sausages and liver.

Note: If pork chops are used rather than lamb these should be started on their own about 5 minutes before the sausages, since they take longer to cook.

Steak with Pineapple

☆ ☆   ① ① ①   ◑

Cooking and preparation time:
20 minutes
SERVES 4

2 tablespoons butter
1 tablespoon chopped parsley
2 teaspoons lemon juice
4 fillet steaks, cut about 1-inch
    thick
freshly ground pepper
4 rings pineapple, fresh or canned
2 tablespoons butter

Mix together 2 tablespoons of butter, parsley and lemon juice. Form the mixture into a square pat, and put it in the refrigerator to chill. If canned pineapple is used then mash 2-3 teaspoonfuls of the juice with the butter, and use only 1 teaspoon lemon juice.
Flatten the steaks until they are a little larger than the rings of pineapple. Cut the steaks across in half leaving one edge uncut; open them out like books.
Sprinkle the inside generously with pepper. Heat the grill [broiler] on a high setting.
Lay a ring of pineapple and a quarter of the chilled flavoured butter on one half of each steak. Fold the other half over and secure it with a toothpick.
Dot each steak with a little butter and an extra sprinkling of pepper, then grill [broil] for approximately 4 minutes. Turn the steaks over, dot them with the rest of the butter, sprinkle them with pepper and grill them for a further 4 minutes.

Serve with creamy mashed potatoes and a green vegetable.

Note: This recipe can be made with bananas in the centre. In this case you slice the bananas and arrange them on one side of the steak before folding the meat over.

Marinated Steak

☆   ① ①   ●

Preparation and cooking time:
30 minutes (including marinating time)
SERVES 4

¾ teaspoon dry mustard
1½ teaspoons vinegar
1½ teaspoons soy sauce
1 teaspoon lemon juice
freshly ground pepper
1½ lbs. rump steak
2 tablespoons butter

Blend together the mustard and vinegar. Add the soy sauce and lemon juice.
Place the steak in a dish, sprinkle it with freshly ground pepper and add the marinade. Leave for about 10 minutes.
Heat the grill [broiler] on a high setting. Turn the steak over in the marinade and leave for a further 10 minutes, then remove from the dish and dot with half the butter.
Grill [broil] for about 5 minutes, turn, dot the steak with the remaining butter and grill it for a further 5 minutes.
Serve with any extra juices poured over it.

Note: the steak can be left in the marinade for a few hours if that is more convenient.

opposite: Marinated Steak, Grilled Lamb Chops with bacon

MINCED BEEF

Minced [ground] beef is one of the most versatile of meats, and any cook on a budget knows at least half a dozen ways of serving it attractively. Here, three more dishes to add to your repertoire—two of which are rather special, and another for every day. You might like to use the stuffing mixture for the Stuffed Cabbage Leaves in vine leaves, as well. The Savoury Mince is used in the Beef Cobbler, but could also be topped with creamed potato and browned, or on its own make a meat sauce for pasta.

below: Meatballs in Piquant Sauce

Savoury Mince

☆   ①   ⚫

Preparation and cooking time:
30 minutes
S E R V E S 4 in a main dish

1 medium-sized onion
1 clove of garlic
2 tablespoons butter
1 lb. minced [ground] beef
1 lb. canned tomatoes
2 tablespoons tomato purée
1 teaspoon sugar
salt and pepper
½ teaspoon dried basil or oregano

Peel and chop the onion; peel and crush the garlic. Fry the onion and garlic in the butter until the onion is transparent, then add the beef and continue to cook, stirring occasionally, until the beef has browned and is crumbly.
Add the tomatoes, breaking them up with a fork. the purée, sugar, salt, pepper, and herbs, and bring to the boil, stirring. Reduce the heat, cover, and simmer for about 30 minutes or until the mixture has thickened and the flavours have combined.

Greek Cabbage Rolls

☆ ☆ ☆ ①   ⚫

Preparation and cooking time:
30 minutes
S E R V E S 4

2 onions
1-2 tablespoons oil
¼ lb. mushrooms
1 lb. minced [ground] beef
salt and freshly ground black pepper
½ pint [1¼ cups] stock
8 large cabbage leaves
1 egg
4 oz. [1 cup] cooked rice
4 tablespoons butter
2 tablespoons flour
½ pint [1¼ cups] yogurt
2 tablespoons tomato purée
2 teaspoons sugar
juice of ½ a lemon

Heat oven to 350°F (Gas Mark 4, 180°C).
Peel and chop the onions. Heat the oil in a saucepan and sauté the onions lightly.

Meanwhile wash, dry and chop the mushrooms, add them to the onions with the minced beef, salt and pepper, and cook, stirring until browned. Add about half the stock, bring to the boil, cover, reduce the heat and simmer for about 10 minutes.
Boil the cabbage leaves in salted water until they are softened. (When bent they should not break.) Drain, and smooth each leaf out on a flat surface, cutting away the thick end of the stalk. Mix the egg and rice into the minced beef mixture and adjust the seasoning. Spoon about 2-3 tablespoons of meat mixture on to each cabbage leaf, roll up the leaves turning in the ends and secure them with a toothpick. Melt half the butter, and sauté the cabbage rolls on all sides.
Carefully remove the toothpicks and pack the cabbage rolls tightly in a heat-proof dish.
Melt the remaining butter and make a sauce with the flour and remaining stock. Add the remaining ingredients and salt and pepper to taste. Bring the sauce to the boil, stirring, then pour over cabbage rolls and bake for about 10 minutes.

Minced Beef Cobbler

☆ ☆   ①   ⚫

Preparation and cooking time:
30 minutes (using cooked minced [ground] beef)
S E R V E S 4

1 lb. prepared savoury mince
14 oz. [3½ cups] self-raising flour
½ teaspoon salt
4 tablespoons butter
2 tablespoons milk and a little water
beaten egg to glaze

Heat oven to 450°F (Gas Mark 8, 230°C)
Put the prepared savoury mince into a heat-proof dish.
To prepare the topping, sift the flour and salt into a bowl and rub in the butter until the mixture resembles breadcrumbs. Add sufficient milk and water to make a scone-like dough (just enough liquid to make the mixture form a ball, and leave the sides of the bowl clean).

Roll out the dough and cut into circles of 1½—2-inches diameter. Arrange the circles around the edge of the dish, overlapping them slightly.
Brush the tops with beaten egg and put into the oven for about 20 minutes or until golden brown.

Meatballs in Piquant Sauce

☆ ☆   ①   ⚫

Preparation and cooking time:
30 minutes
S E R V E S 4

1 small onion
1 lb. lean minced [ground] beef
1 teaspoon chopped fresh mint
1 tablespoon chopped parsley
1 tablespoon cooked rice
**   or fresh breadcrumbs**
salt and pepper
15 fl. oz. [2 cups] beef stock
½ pint [1¼ cups] water
2 egg yolks
juice of 1 lemon

Peel and cut the onion into wedges.
Mince [grind] the beef one extra time with the onion, if possible. If you do not have a mincer [meat grinder], chop the onion finely and mix it thoroughly with the beef.
Mix the beef and onion with the mint, parsley, rice or breadcrumbs, salt and pepper to taste, and about 3 tablespoons of the beef stock. Put the remaining stock, and the water to boil in a large saucepan.
Meanwhile, with wet hands, form the meat mixture into small balls about the size of half a walnut.
Drop the prepared meat balls into the stock and boil them for about 20 minutes. Drain and keep hot on a serving dish.
Beat the egg yolks together with the lemon juice. Slowly add some of the hot stock, beating constantly. Stir the egg yolk mixture into the remaining stock. Cover it and let it stand for 5 minutes off the heat. Serve the meat balls either with the sauce poured over them or served separately, and garnished with chopped parsley. Serve with rice or noodles.

Note: If preferred, the meat balls can be made larger, about the size of a walnut. They will then take about 40 minutes to cook.

FRITTERS

If correctly made fritters are a delightfully light yet satisfying dish—but if badly cooked they become unpleasantly heavy and greasy. Always make sure that the fat for deep-frying has been pre-heated to the correct temperature, so that no fat is absorbed by the batter.

Fritters are often served as a dessert, although the Cheese Puff recipe is a savoury exception to the rule, which may be served as a supper dish. For sweet fritters try using a selection of other fruits, such as pieces of pineapple or banana—or even thinly sliced banana sandwich fritters.

below: fritters in preparation

Apple Fritters

☆ ☆　① 🍋

Preparation and cooking time:
25 minutes
S E R V E S 4

4 oz. [1 cup] flour
2 tablespoons castor [fine] sugar
2 egg yolks
1 tablespoon butter, melted and
 cooled
2½ fl. oz. beer or cider
2½ fl. oz. water
3 medium apples
1 egg white
deep fat for frying

Sift the flour and sugar, make a well
in the centre and add the egg yolks
and the melted butter. Gradually add
the liquid, mixing it all into a smooth
batter and beat well.
Peel and core the apples and cut into
even sized chunks.
Stiffly whisk the egg white and gently
fold into the batter.
Heat the deep fat—it is the correct
temperature when a drop of batter
immediately rises to the surface and
begins to brown. Dip each apple piece
into the batter and, making sure it is
thoroughly coated, drop it into the hot
fat and fry until it is puffed up and
golden brown. Drain on absorbent
paper. Continue to fry the apple
fritters this way, and serve them
sprinkled with castor [fine] sugar.
Serve with fruit purée or whipped
cream flavoured with a liqueur.

Variation:
Sift ½ teaspoon of powdered
cinnamon or mixed spice [allspice]
with the flour and sugar, or add a
little grated lemon rind to the batter
before folding in the egg white.

Cheese Puffs

☆ ☆　①　🍲

Preparation and cooking time:
30 minutes
S E R V E S 4

5 oz. [1¼ cups] plain [all-purpose]
 flour
4 oz. [½ cup] butter
½ pt. [1¼ cups] water
4 eggs
4 oz. [1 cup] finely chopped

Gruyère cheese (or any similar
 hard cheese)
salt and a pinch cayenne pepper
deep fat for frying
grated Parmesan cheese

Sift the flour. Melt the butter in a
saucepan. Add the water and bring to
the boil. When bubbling, remove the
pan from the heat and add all the
flour at once. Beat until smooth and
cool. Gradually beat in the eggs,
continuing to beat until the mixture
is smooth and glossy. Stir in the
cheese and salt and a pinch of
cayenne pepper.
Heat the deep fat to fry the cheese
puffs. The temperature is right when
a very faint blue haze rises from the
surface. Carefully drop a spoonful of
the cheese mixture into the hot fat,
frying 2—3 puffs at a time, and so
allowing room for them to rise. Fry
the puffs until well-risen and golden
brown which will take about 5—7
minutes per batch. Remove from the
fat with a draining spoon and drain
on absorbent paper. Keep them hot
in a cool oven while frying the rest
of the mixture.
These must be served very hot, dusted
with a little grated Parmesan cheese,
and accompanied by well seasoned,
thick tomato sauce.

Note: Cheese puffs may be served as
a supper dish with a mixed salad or
as a first course of a meal, in which
case the mixture should be fried
in teaspoonfuls.

Date and Almond
Fritters

☆ ☆　①　🍲

Preparation and cooking time:
30 minutes
S E R V E S 4—6

4 oz. [1 cup] of all-purpose batter
dates
blanched almonds
deep fat for frying
castor [fine] sugar

Make the batter (see page 62).
Remove the stones from the dates and
replace them with skinned almonds.
Dip into the prepared batter and fry
immediately in the deep fat until
puffed and golden. Drain on

absorbent paper and keep warm while
completing the frying of the fritters.
To serve: Dredge with castor [fine]
sugar and serve with lightly whipped
double [heavy] cream.

Orange Fritters

☆ ☆　①　🍲

Preparation and cooking time:
30 minutes
S E R V E S 4

4 oz. [1 cup] all-purpose batter
3 oranges
Curaçao
deep fat for frying
castor [fine] sugar

Make up the batter [see page 62].
Peel the oranges carefully, removing
all the pith and pips. Slice the
oranges, and marinate them for a few
minutes in Curaçao.
Heat the deep fat until a drop of
batter will rise immediately to the
surface and begin to brown. Just
before cooking fold the stiffly beaten
egg white into the batter. Drain the
orange slices, reserving the Curaçao,
and dip them in the batter to coat
them completely. Fry them in the
deep fat, turning them over with a
spatula until they are golden brown
and puffed. Drain on absorbent
paper and keep hot in the oven,
while frying the rest of the fritters.
Dredge the fritters with castor [fine]
sugar and serve with a whipped sauce.

Whipped sauce:
2 tablespoons icing [confectioners']
 sugar
1 egg yolk
1 egg
2 tablespoons Curaçao

Place all the ingredients in a bowl.
Stand the bowl over a pan of slowly
boiling water and whisk the sauce
until thick, light and frothy. Serve
immediately.

Variations:
§ In place of the oranges, use sliced
bananas, soaked in rum, instead of
Curaçao, or peeled, halved, stoned
and quartered peaches soaked in a
little brandy.
§ Use the liqueur in which the fruit
has been marinating in the whipped
sauce, and omit the Curacao.

WAFFLES

Waffles are always popular, and are very easy to cook if the necessary preparations are carried out. The iron must always be pre-heated for 10-15 minutes before cooking begins, so that there is time for the correct temperature to be stabilized. And the iron must be brushed thoroughly with oil before any batter is poured in—too little oil and the waffle will stick; too much and there will be grease spots on the surface of the waffles. If you own an electric waffle iron remember to cook the waffles according to the manufacturer's specific instructions for his equipment.

Sand Waffles

☆ ☆ ☆ ① ⬤

Preparation and cooking time:
30 minutes
S E R V E S 6-7 fillings of a heart-
    shaped waffle iron

2 oz. [½ cup] **cornflour** [cornstarch]
8 oz. [2 cups] **flour**
½ teaspoon **salt**
½ teaspoon **ground cinnamon**
4 oz. [½ cup] **butter or margarine**
2 **eggs**
2 oz. [4 tablespoons] **castor** [fine]
    sugar
4 tablespoons **sour cream**
12 fl. oz. [1½ cups] **milk**
grated rind of ½ a lemon
a little oil for brushing the iron

Sift together the cornflour, flour, salt and cinnamon. Cream the fat with the sugar. Beat the eggs and mix them into the fat and sugar mixture with a little of the sifted flour. Gradually add the rest of the flour mixture with the sour cream and milk, to form a fairly thick but pouring batter. Stir in the grated lemon rind and beat the batter well.
Bake one test waffle, and if the batter is too thick add a little lukewarm

water. When the batter is of the correct consistency, spoon it into the waffle iron, press the lid down firmly and bake for a few minutes until golden brown and crisp. Turn the waffles on to a wire rack and serve them hot.
Serve with a bowl of whipped cream flavoured with a little Kirsch, or whipped cream and a jug of warmed maple syrup or honey and a few lemon wedges.

Rum Waffles

☆ ☆ ☆ ① ⬤

Preparation and cooking time:
20-30 minutes
S E R V E S 6-7 fillings of a heart-
    shaped waffle iron

4 oz. [½ cup] **butter or margarine**
2 oz. [4 tablespoons] **soft brown**
    sugar
2 **eggs**
8 oz. [2 cups] **flour**
2 oz. [½ cup] **cornflour** [cornstarch]
½ teaspoon **salt**
2 teaspoons **baking powder**
18 fl. oz. [2¼ cups] **milk**
3 tablespoons **rum**
a little oil for brushing the iron

Cream the fat and sugar. Beat the eggs and add to the mixture with a little of the sifted flour. Beat all well together. Add the rest of the flour with the cornflour, salt, baking powder and the milk and rum to make a fairly thin batter.
If the batter is too thick, add a little lukewarm water rather than milk, as water makes the waffles crisper.
Fill the waffle iron with a few spoonfuls of the prepared batter, press the lid down well and cook on both sides over a medium heat for a few minutes. The waffles should be browned and crisp. Turn the waffles on to a wire rack and keep

them warm but never pile them on top of each other.
Serve the rum waffles hot with cream.

Waffle Horns

☆ ☆ ☆ ① ⬤

Preparation and cooking time:
30 minutes
M A K E S about 24 horns

4 tablespoons **castor** [fine] **sugar**
18 fl. oz. [2¼ cups] **water**
4 oz. [½ cup] **butter or margarine**
2 **eggs**
8 oz. [2 cups] **flour**
2 oz. [½ cup] **cornflour** [cornstarch]
½ teaspoon **salt**
1 teaspoon **vanilla essence**
a little oil for brushing the iron

Dissolve the castor sugar in the water over the heat then remove from the heat and cool. Cream the fat until soft and beat the eggs into it until well blended. Add the flour and cornflour sifted together with the salt, and gradually mix in the cooled water and sugar mixture. Mix well. Flavour with the vanilla essence. Leave to stand for 10-15 minutes. This batter has to be thin so that the waffles may be curled into horns.
Spoon a little batter on to the horn waffle iron, remembering that a thin waffle is required. Press down the lid firmly. Bake the waffle and roll it up on the waffle iron while it is still hot, with the help of a fork. Work quickly as it will cool very fast and become brittle and break. Leave it to cool and firm up on a wire rack.

To serve when cold: Fill the horns with cream and fruit, as liked, or serve them dusted with sifted icing [confectioners'] sugar as an accompaniment to coffee.

opposite: a selection of waffles

ICE-CREAMS

Ice-creams with added flavour—here we have suggested ways to make bought ice-cream into special desserts, as well as how to prepare your own. And try out your own ideas for accompaniments—a strawberry, peach or banana purée with the Mixed Ice; a canned raspberry purée with the Almond Ice. Or just enjoy them as we have suggested—the delicious contrast between a hot sauce and a cold ice-cream is a delight all will enjoy.

Coffee Ice

☆ ① ●

Preparation and Cooking time:
10 minutes
SERVES 4-6

1¼ pts. [3 cups] **strong black coffee**
5 fl. oz. **double [heavy] cream**
1 tablespoon **vanilla sugar**
1 **family block vanilla ice-cream**
flaked chocolate

Make the coffee and chill it well in the refrigerator. Beat the cream until it is stiff and sweeten it with the vanilla sugar. Half-fill four tall glasses with the chilled coffee. Add cubes of vanilla ice-cream, and crown with a whirl of the whipped cream and flakes of chocolate.
Serve with a straw and a spoon.

Mixed Ice

☆ ☆ ① ① ●

Preparation and cooking time:
30 minutes
SERVES 4-6

½ pint [1¼ cups] **double [heavy] cream**
3 tablespoons **apricot purée, made from well drained canned apricots**
4 tablespoons **icing [confectioners'] sugar**
3 tablespoons **raspberry purée, made from frozen or fresh raspberries**

4 oz. **macaroons**
a little brandy
To decorate:
2½ fl. oz. **double [heavy] cream, stiffly beaten**
flaked chocolate

Whip half of the cream until it begins to stiffen. Add the apricot purée and whip together until thick. Stir in half the sugar. Pour into a suitable container and freeze. Whip the rest of the cream until it begins to stiffen, add the raspberry purée and whip them together until thick. Stir in the rest of the sugar. Pour into a suitable container and freeze.
Line plates or glass bowls with the macaroons which have previously been dipped in the brandy. Place spoonfuls of the ice-cream into the bowls. Pipe with the stiffly beaten cream and crumble the flaked chocolate over the top.

Vanilla Ice with Hot Sauce

☆ ① ◑

Preparation and cooking time:
15 minutes
SERVES 4-6

4-6 **canned pear halves**
6 oz. [¾ cup] **castor [fine] sugar**
2 oz. [½ cup] **walnut halves**
For the chocolate sauce:
3 oz. [¾ cup] **cocoa powder**
3 oz. [½ cup] **soft brown sugar**
3 oz. **castor [⅜ cup fine] sugar**
1 teaspoon **coffee essence**
2 tablespoons **butter**
½ pint [1¼ cups] **milk**
1 **family block of vanilla ice-cream**

Drain the pears very well. Put the sugar in a small heavy pan, and melt it, stirring all the time. Do not let it brown. Spear a walnut with a thin skewer and dip it into the melted sugar. Leave it to cool on a plate. Repeat this process with all the walnuts.
Make the chocolate sauce. Place all the sauce ingredients in a pan. Stir them over a very low heat, until the sugar has dissolved. Bring to the boil slowly. Boil the sauce for a few minutes, until it coats the back of the spoon.
Divide the ice-cream between individual glasses, and place the pear halves on top. Garnish with the nuts

and pour over the hot chocolate sauce. *Serve* at once.

Variation:
Hot butterscotch sauce
1 tablespoon **cornflour [cornstarch]**
5 fl. oz. [⅝ cup] **milk**
4 oz. [½ cup] **dark brown sugar**
2 tablespoons **butter**
Mix the cornflour with a little of the milk to a smooth paste. Place the remainder of the milk with the sugar and butter in a saucepan. Stir over low heat until the sugar dissolves. Pour this on to the cornflour mixture and return it to the pan. Cook, stirring, until it boils and thickens. Serve the sauce hot.

Almond Ice

☆ ☆ ① ① ●

Preparation and cooking time:
30 minutes
SERVES 4-6

5 oz. [1¼ cups] **unpeeled almonds**
5 oz. [⅝ cup] **castor [fine] sugar**
1 **family-sized block of ice-cream**

To make the almond praline, place the nuts and sugar in a heavy-based saucepan. Heat gently; stirring with a metal spoon when the sugar has melted and is beginning to turn to caramel. Continue to stir until the almonds are toasted on all sides. Turn the mixture on to an oiled tin or plate, and leave it to cool.
When the praline has set crush it into pieces with a rolling pin, and pass it through a nut-mill or a grater. Place the ice-cream in a bowl and gently break it up with a fork. Fold in the praline, reserving a few tablespoons of it to decorate the top of the ice-cream.
Pack the ice-cream back into a plastic container, cover it with waxed or greaseproof paper and return it to the freezer or freezing compartment of the refrigerator.
To serve, scoop the ice-cream into individual glasses and sprinkle it with the remainder of the praline.

Note: If the praline is made in advance, it may be kept in an airtight tin until required.

opposite: back: Almond Ice, Coffee Ice, Mixed Ice
front: Vanilla Ice with Hot Sauce

FRUIT DESSERTS

left: *Cream Cake with Raspberries*
below: *Fresh Fruit Salad*

Fruit is always a great standby for meals-in-a-hurry—and a selection of seasonal fruit with cheese makes an attractive end to any meal. But sometimes when good fruit is available in the shops you will want to serve a dish just a little more special. The Cream Cake with Raspberries tastes as good as it looks—and could of course be served with frozen or canned raspberries as well. Try the Strawberry Baked Alaska with other fruits: apricots, bananas or blackberries would all be delicious. And almost any fruits could be added to the Fresh Fruit Salad, for extra flavour and contrast.

Fresh Fruit Salad

Preparation and cooking time:
20 minutes
SERVES 8

1 lb. [2 cups] **sugar**
½ pint [1¼ cups] **water**
2 **lemons**
2 **oranges**
2 **apples**
1 **pear**
1 **banana**
small bunch **black grapes**
small bunch **green grapes**
¼ lb. **strawberries**
½ small **pineapple**
4 tablespoons **Kirsch or Curaçao**

Put the sugar and water into a heavy based saucepan. Remove the zest (cut thinly) from the lemons, and add this to the sugar and water. Bring to the boil slowly, stirring occasionally, and boil for 5 minutes. Leave in the saucepan while preparing the oranges.
Remove the peel and pith from oranges, cutting thickly, and cut the flesh into rings. Place these in a suitable bowl, and strain the syrup over the oranges.
Squeeze the juice from the lemons and add this to the oranges and syrup. Then, adding each fruit to the bowl as it is prepared, peel and core the apples and cut in slices, or into more chunky pieces. If you have attractive red apples, leave half of one unpeeled and slice this into the fruit salad for added colour. Peel, core and slice the pear. Peel and slice the bananas.
Wash the grapes and dry on absorbent paper. Cut in half, and remove the pips.
Hull the strawberries, wash and dry,

and either keep whole or cut into slices. Remove the skin from the pineapple, and cut the flesh into chunky pieces. Finally add the Kirsch or Curaçao. Stir gently, chill, and serve.

Cream Cake with Raspberries

Preparation and cooking time:
20 minutes
SERVES 4-6

8 oz. [2 cups] **flour**
6 oz. [¾ cup] **butter**
3 tablespoons **double [heavy] cream**
For the filling:
double [heavy] cream
fresh or frozen raspberries

Heat oven to 400°F (Gas Mark 6, 200°C).
Sift the flour into a large bowl. Rub in the butter, until the mixture resembles fine breadcrumbs. Add the cream and blend the ingredients together to form a stiff dough.
Roll out the dough and cut it into two rounds, each about 10 inches in diameter. Prick the dough all over, place the rounds on two large baking sheets, sprinkle them with sugar and bake them in the oven for about 10 minutes or until the pastry is beginning to colour slightly.
Leave them for a few minutes on the baking sheet to harden, and then transfer them on to a serving plate. Whip the double cream until stiff. Sandwich the two pastry crusts with whipped cream. Serve with a dish of raspberries.

Strawberry Baked Alaska

Preparation and cooking time:
30 minutes
SERVES 6-8

1 bought **7-inch sponge base**
2 **egg whites**
4 oz. **icing [scant 1 cup confectioners' sugar**

½-¾ lb. **strawberries**
small block of **strawberry ice-cream**

Heat oven to 450°F (Gas Mark 8, 230°C).
Whisk together the egg whites and sugar until they form stiff peaks. Remove the hulls from the strawberries, and slice the berries neatly.
Place the sponge cake on to a baking tray and cover it with the strawberry slices. Now place the block of ice-cream on top and, working quickly, cut and spread it to fit the sponge base. Then cover the whole with the meringue mixture, making sure that no gaps have been left.
Bake for just a few minutes until the peaks of meringue turn golden. Serve immediately.

Oranges in Syrup

Preparation and cooking time:
25 minutes
SERVES 6

¾ lb. **castor [1½ cups fine] sugar**
½ pint [1¼ cups] **water**
6 **oranges**
1 **lemon**
small piece of **cinnamon stick**
2 fl. oz. **orange Curaçao, Grand Marnier or Kirsch**

Put the sugar and water into a heavy based saucepan, and stir them over a low heat until the sugar has completely dissolved. Boil uncovered, for 10 minutes.
Meanwhile peel the oranges thinly and cut off and discard the white pith. Slice the oranges into rings, or remove each orange segment with a sharp knife and put them into a bowl.
After the sugar and water has boiled remove it from heat and add all the orange peel except one piece. Grate the lemon peel into the syrup, squeeze the juice and add it with the cinnamon stick, to the syrup. Stir and allow to cool for a few minutes.
Cut the reserved peel into fine shreds for decoration.
Strain the syrup over the orange slices, pressing the peel in the sifter with a wooden spoon so that no syrup is wasted.
Sprinkle with the shreds of peel and liqueur and chill.
Serve with cream or ice cream, and sponge finger biscuits [cookies].

CREAMY DESSERTS

Although there are many pre-packaged instant desserts on the market today—often a great help when quick meals are needed—their flavours tend to be a little bland for our palates. Something which can be whipped up in minutes, yet still retain an individual touch, is what's needed. Here four recipes solve the problem in especially tasty ways. Both the Orange Delight and Melon Dessert use fresh ingredients with canned or packet foods, while the Chocolate Mousse adds spirit to an old favourite. The Baked Custards provide a soothing and simple flavour that should please everyone.

Individual Baked Custards

☆   ①   ⏰

Preparation and cooking time:
30 minutes
SERVES 6

1 tablespoon butter
1 pint [2½ cups] milk
2 eggs
1 egg yolk
1½ oz. [3 tablespoons] castor [fine] sugar
pinch salt
½ teaspoon vanilla essence or a little grated nutmeg

Heat oven to 325°F (Gas Mark 3, 170°C).
Lightly butter the insides of 6 custard cups. Place them in a baking tin.
Heat the milk gently in a saucepan over a low heat. Put all the remaining ingredients (except the grated nutmeg) in a bowl and mix well with a fork.
When small bubbles appear at the edges of the milk, pour it on to the egg mixture, slowly at first, blending with a fork. Strain into the prepared custard cups.
Have ready a kettle of boiling water. Place the baking tin of filled custard cups in the oven, and fill it to half way up the sides of the custard cups with hot water. Bake for about 25 minutes,

or until a knife inserted into the centre of a custard comes out clean. Remove from the oven and cool.
Baked custards are delicious with stewed fruits, and caramel, chocolate or fruit sauces. They are also excellent with sponge fingers or almond biscuits [cookies].

Chocolate Mousse

☆   ① ①   ⏰

Preparation and cooking time:
15 minutes
SERVES 4

6 oz. plain [semi-sweet] chocolate
3 eggs, separated
1 tablespoon whisky or rum (optional)
To decorate:
crystallized violets
5 fl. oz. double [heavy] cream, stiffly whipped

Place the chocolate in a bowl over a saucepan of simmering water. Whisk the egg whites until stiff.
When the chocolate is melted, remove from the heat and beat in the egg yolks, one at a time, and the whisky or rum. Fold in the whisked egg whites, and pour the chocolate mousse into one shallow dish or into individual ones. Leave to set in the refrigerator.
Just before serving decorate with crystallized violets and pipe with whipped cream.

Melon Dessert

☆ ☆   ①   ⏰

Preparation time:
15 minutes
SERVES 4

½ a honeydew melon
1 small glass Kirsch
1 grapefruit
about 12 canned cherries
½ pint [1¼ cups] double [heavy] cream
1 tablespoon icing [confectioners'] sugar
a few drops vanilla essence

Remove the melon flesh from the skin

with a cutter which makes ball shapes, or chop it into cubes. Remove any left-over fruit from the skin, and chop finely. Put all the flesh into a bowl and pour the Kirsch over it.
Remove all peel and white pith from the grapefruit and cut each section out, leaving behind the pith and discarding all the pips. Add the flesh to the melon. Remove all the stones [pits] from the cherries. (If you use a special device, this may be done so that the cherries remain whole.) Add these to the melon and grapefruit mixture and chill them.
Whisk the cream until thick, and add the sugar and vanilla to it. Arrange the fruit mixture attractively just before serving, and pipe the cream on top. Serve with sponge fingers, and decorate with slivers of almonds.

Orange Delight

☆ ☆   ① ①   ⏰

Preparation and cooking time:
20 minutes plus setting time
SERVES 6

1 orange flavoured jelly [jello] sufficient for 15 fl. oz. [2 cups] liquid
5 fl. oz. water
1 tablespoon Curaçao (or fresh orange juice)
3 eggs
3 oz. [⅜ cup] castor [fine] sugar
1 orange
pistachio nuts

Dissolve the jelly in 5 fl. oz. water. Add the Curaçao or orange juice and cool the jelly until it is just on the point of setting. Meanwhile, whisk the eggs and sugar over hot but not boiling water, until the mixture falls, leaving a trail for a few seconds, when the whisk is lifted just above the bowl.
When the jelly is just on the point of setting, fold it into the eggs and sugar mixture and blend them gently but thoroughly. Pour it into a bowl and chill. When chilled turn out the dessert on to a serving dish.
Remove the skin from the orange, peeling thickly, and cut each segment out leaving behind the pith. Decorate the orange dessert with the segments of orange, and the pistachios.

opposite: top: Chocolate Mousse
front: Orange Delight, Melon Dessert

BASIC RECIPES & METHODS

Pizza Dough

Preparation time: *1 hour*
MAKES 8 oz.

8 oz. [2 cups] flour
1 teaspoon salt
3 tablespoons butter
4 tablespoons lukewarm water
4 tablespoons lukewarm milk
½ oz. fresh baker's yeast or 2
    teaspoons dried yeast
1 teaspoon sugar

Sift the flour and salt into a warmed bowl. Rub the butter into the flour. Cream the yeast and sugar together and add to the lukewarm liquids. (If you use dried yeast, dissolve the sugar in the water and sprinkle the yeast on the top. Leave for 5 minutes until it begins to bubble then add the milk to it.)
Add the yeast mixture to the flour and beat thoroughly. Cover and leave to rise in a warm place until double its bulk: this will take about 40 minutes.
Flour the dough and pat into shape with the fist, on to a large floured baking sheet, or it may be rolled into any shape with a rolling pin.

All Purpose Batter

Preparation time:
5 to 10 minutes

4 oz. [1 cup] flour
a good pinch baking powder
2 tablespoons castor [fine] sugar
2 eggs, separated
5 fl. oz. milk and water
1 tablespoon melted butter, cooled

Sift the flour, baking powder and sugar into a bowl. Make a well in the centre of the flour and drop in the egg yolks. Gradually mix in the liquid and the cooled melted butter. Beat the

batter until smooth. Just before the batter is to be used, fold in the stiffly beaten egg whites.

Basic Omelette

Preparation and cooking time:
5 minutes
SERVES 2

3 eggs
salt and freshly ground pepper
butter

Beat or whisk the eggs with a fork, to blend the yolks and whites thoroughly. Add salt and pepper to taste. Heat the omelette pan and add the butter, waiting until the heat is sufficient to melt and 'foam' the butter. Tilt the pan so the butter covers the bottom and sides of the pan. When the foam has almost subsided and the butter just starts to colour, pour in the eggs.
With a fork or spatula pull the edges of the egg mass towards the centre, as it thickens. The liquid part then runs into spaces. Repeat this until there is no more liquid but the egg is still soft and moist in appearance.
Spoon on any prepared filling. Lift the handle of the pan so that the omelette slides over on to a warmed plate. Dot with a little extra butter and serve immediately.

Variations:
Lightly mix one of the selected flavours into the prepared eggs before cooking.
§ *Cheese:* 3 oz. [¾ cup] grated cheese.
§ *Parsley:* 1 tablespoon finely chopped parsley.
§ *Herb:* Add 1 tablespoon of one of the following herbs: chopped fresh oregano, thyme, basil, mint, tarragon, chives, parsley or dill.

§ *Ham:* Add less salt to the eggs and mix in 1 oz. [2 tablespoons] of chopped ham.

Pancake Batter

Preparation and cooking time:
20 minutes
MAKES about 12 pancakes

4 oz. [1 cup] flour
½ teaspoon salt
2 eggs
½ pint [1¼ cups] milk
1 tablespoon melted butter

Sift the flour and salt into a large bowl. Make a well in the centre, and drop the eggs into it with a little of the milk and the butter. Mix this to a smooth batter, and when there are no lumps at all add a little more of the milk and mix again. When all of the milk has been added beat very well and then leave to one side for a few minutes, before making pancakes.

French Fritter Batter

Preparation time: *10 minutes*
MAKES about 14 fritters

4 oz [½ cup] flour
¼ teaspoon baking powder
¼ teaspoon salt
1 egg, separated
5 fl. oz. milk
2 tablespoons oil and 2 tablespoons
    butter for frying

Sift the flour, salt and baking powder into a bowl. Make a well in the centre and drop in the egg yolk.
Gradually add the milk a little at a time, mixing well with each new addition. When all the milk has been added beat well again to produce an even batter.

Add flavouring ingredients at this stage, then whisk the egg white until stiff and fold it into the batter just before using.

Note: Single [light] cream may be used instead of milk, for a richer batter.

Variations:
§ *Corn Fritters.* Add ¼ teaspoon paprika with dry ingredients, and 6 ounces [1 cup] of drained cooked corn to the batter.
§ Very small pieces of any well-flavoured ingredient may be used, such as kidney, bacon, or corned beef.

Making Fritters
Heat the oil and butter together in a frying pan, and drop scant tablespoonfuls of the mixture into the pan. Fry until golden brown underneath, then turn and fry on the other side. This process should take about 5 minutes for one fritter; do not try to hurry it.

Thick Tomato Sauce

Preparation and cooking time:
30 minutes
MAKES about ½ pint [1¼ cups]

2 tablespoons butter
1 small onion peeled and chopped
2 tablespoons flour
8 fl. oz. [1 cup] stock or water .
a good pinch of mixed herbs
salt, pepper and a pinch sugar
12 fl. oz. [1½ cups] canned
     tomatoes
1 teaspoon tomato purée

Melt the butter, and gently sauté the chopped onion until transparent. Remove from the heat, sprinkle in the flour, blend in the stock or water, and add the herbs, seasonings, canned

tomatoes and purée. Blend well together. Return to the heat, bring to the boil, stirring constantly, and simmer for about 20 minutes. Strain. *Adjust* the seasoning if necessary, reheat, and serve.

Oriental Sauce

Preparation and cooking time:
10 minutes
MAKES about 8 fl. oz.

2 tablespoons soy sauce
5 fl. oz. stock or water
1 tablespoon cornflour [cornstarch]
1 tablespoon brown sugar
1 tablespoon Worcestershire sauce
1 level teaspoon made mustard
1 tablespoon vinegar
a dash of Tabasco sauce

Mix all the ingredients together well in a saucepan. Bring to the boil, cook for a few minutes and serve hot.

Quick Chutney

Preparation and cooking time:
10 minutes
MAKES 4 servings

2 large pickled gherkins
1 tablespoon apricot jam
1 teaspoon soy sauce
2 teaspoons Worcestershire sauce
1 teaspoon capers
1 teaspoon tomato ketchup
2 teaspoons juice from canned fruit
     (use peach or pineapple juice)

Chop the gherkins, and any whole apricot pieces in the jam and mix well with the rest of the ingredients, adding more fruit juice if necessary. Serve with grilled [broiled] meat, in sandwiches or with toast snacks (see page 5).

Chunky Apple Chutney

Preparation and cooking time:
25 minutes
MAKES 6 servings

4 medium-sized cooking apples
5 oz [⅝ cup] sugar
½ pint [1¼ cups] water
¼ teaspoon salt
¼ teaspoon ground ginger
6 tablespoons fruit chutney

Wash and core the apples, and cut them into large chunks. Place the sugar, water, salt and ginger into a saucepan, mix well, and bring to the boil. Add the apple chunks, reduce the heat, and simmer uncovered for about 10 minutes or until the apple is tender.
Remove the apple chunks carefully from the pan, and boil the syrup again until it has reduced and thickened a little more. Add the fruit chutney, mix well and then combine this with the apple chunks. Serve cold with curries or other spicy dishes.

Cranberry Orange Sauce

Preparation and cooking time:
15 minutes
MAKES ½ pint [1¼ cups]

½ lb. fresh cranberries
3 oz. [⅜ cup] sugar
a scant 5 fl. oz. water
1 tablespoon grated orange zest

Wash the cranberries, drain, and place them in a saucepan with the sugar and water. Bring to the boil, reduce the heat and simmer covered for about 8 minutes until the skins break. Add the orange zest and allow to cool.
Serve with poultry and other meats. It is especially good with baked ham.